ORGANIZATIONAL
CHANGE
THROUGH
EFFECTIVE
LEADERSHIP

ORGANIZATIONAL CHANGE THROUGH EFFECTIVE LEADERSHIP

second edition

Robert H. Guest
The Amos Tuck School
 of Business Administration
Dartmouth College

Paul Hersey
California American University

Kenneth H. Blanchard
University of Massachusetts

Prentice-Hall, Englewood Cliffs, New Jersey 07632

Library of Congress Cataloging-in-Publication Data

GUEST, ROBERT H.
  Organizational change through effective leadership.

  Bibliography: p.
  Includes index.
  1. Organizational change—Case studies.
I. Hersey, Paul.   II. Blanchard, Kenneth H.
III. Title.
HD58.8.G83 1986   658.4′06′0722   85-28136
ISBN 0-13-641390-0

Editorial/production supervision
and interior design: Pamela Wilder
Cover design: Diane Saxe
Manufacturing buyer: Ed O'Dougherty

Printed in the United States of America

10   9   8   7   6   5   4

ISBN 0-13-641390-0 01

Prentice-Hall International (UK) Limited, *London*
Prentice-Hall of Australia Pty. Limited, *Sydney*
Prentice-Hall Canada Inc., *Toronto*
Prentice-Hall Hispanoamericana, S.A., *Mexico*
Prentice-Hall of India Private Limited, *New Delhi*
Prentice-Hall of Japan, Inc., *Tokyo*
Prentice-Hall of Southeast Asia Pte. Ltd., *Singapore*
Editora Prentice-Hall do Brasil, Ltda., *Rio de Janeiro*
Whitehall Books Limited, *Wellington, New Zealand*

To KATE
   SUZANNE
   MARGIE

Contents

Preface

Managers in today's complex dynamic organizations must continually face the challenge of change. To cope effectively with this challenge they must be able to diagnose what is going on in the environment, develop strategies for meeting new conditions, then implement a change process that will sustain the health and vitality of their organizations. To carry out such changes requires the imaginative and intelligent management of the most valuable resource of all—the people who spend the greater part of their working hours making their organizations work.

The issue of managing change is the focus of this book. In the first edition the authors used one case study, the Plant Y story, to illuminate both the theory and practice of organizational change. In this edition another case, the Plant Z story, has been added together with an update of new theories and concepts related to leadership and change. Each case is presented separately.

Both cases are real life stories of successful change in two large American plants in two different companies. What we say in the introduction to the Plant Y story applies to both. They are studies of patients who were "actutely ill and who became extremely healthy." The patients were not persons but managements and personnel of large complex organizations. From these words can be deduced the unique features of this book. Although both settings are industrial plants, we know from experience with the first edition that the book is of practical interest to leaders in all kinds of organizations–business, education, health care, military, political, or religious. The authors have conducted research in or consulted a wide variety of organizations and have found that the "message" from these two cases is both clear and appropriate regardless of the institutional setting.

Our feeling, based upon many years of experience dealing with leaders and their organizations, is that there is enormous potential energy and creativity which seems to get stifled by rules, habits, and all the paraphernalia of bureaucracy. The more we move around and talk with people the more we are impressed with the wealth of their constructive ideas. We are then appalled when we observe the actual process of communication and action among bosses, subordinates, and peers as these ideas for change rarely seem to surface. Hence, they cannot be acted upon. The sad conclusion one reaches is that organizations, to use an analogy, are designed to perform as six cylinder engines, yet are only "hitting" on three or four cylinders.

This was true at one time both at Plant Y and Plant Z. In both cases change, leading to remarkable success, was initiated primarily by each respective manager. Essentially the Plant Y story focused on what happened in the *management* sector of the organization with some secondary observations about the behavior of rank and file employees. There were virtually no changes in the basic organizational structure. The primary focus of the Plant Z story, cited by Jerome Rosow of The Work in America Institute as "one of the most successful turnarounds in American industry," is on the *worker* sector and the changes that were generated as a result of worker participation and involvement in the decision-making process. Unlike Plant Y the changes at the worker level at Plant Z were paralleled by substantial changes in the organizational structure and management functions. This participative phenomenon which spread throughout many organizations during the 1970s and 1980s came to be known as the "Quality of Worklife" (QWL) or the "Employee Involvement" (EI) movement.

The American sociologist, Robert Merton, who knew one of these cases, once wrote: "More is learned from a single success than from multiple failures. A single success proves it can be done. Therefore, it is necessary to learn what made it work."

As Merton's remarks imply, although both stories are interesting and valuable in themselves as "success" models, to be even more helpful to practitioners "it is necessary to learn what made [them] work." This book is not merely a narrative study of two cases but contains theoretical, diagnostic, and therepeutic materials as well. The patients *"become extremely healthy."* In fact, the main reason for sharing these two case studies is to illustrate how behavioral science theory and research may be helpful to practicing managers in diagnosing human situations and in carrying through strategies for change. Thus, the text attempts to integrate both theory and practice in such a way as to support the old adage attributed to Kurt Lewin, "There is nothing so practical as a good theory."

ROBERT H. GUEST
PAUL HERSEY
KENNETH H. BLANCHARD

ORGANIZATIONAL
CHANGE
THROUGH
EFFECTIVE
LEADERSHIP

part I
THE PLANT Y CASE

chapter
1

Setting the Stage

I. INTRODUCTION

What follows is a longitudinal study of change in a large assembly plant, which we shall call "Plant Y."[1] This is a study of a patient who was acutely ill and who became extremely healthy. The "patient" was not a person but a management, the management of a large, complex, industrial organization. It is a study of the process of change, not only in attitudes but also in the pattern of actions and relations, which, in the span of three years, measurably altered the performance of the entire organization.

This case study is unique in several aspects. First, it describes a real life experience in a real organization covering many dimensions of reality. In short, we will be examining a whole system, not isolating one dimension of reality or organizational life. In fact, as the Plant Y story unfolds, we will continually be touching on all the elements in the system that explained what happened.

Second, it is one of the few systematic studies of a large complex organization in process of change. This real life case not only gives "before and after" data on the organization studied, but focuses on the process of change itself—how Plant Y moved from a condition of failure compared with five other almost identical plants in its division to a condition of success. This case study adds, in other words, the longitudinal dimension to a study of organizational behavior undergoing change.

---

[1] The data for this case study was generated from research conducted by Robert H. Guest and his colleagues when he was working at the Technology Project, Yale Institute of Human Relations. It was first published as Robert H. Guest, *Organizational Change: The Effect of Successful Leadership* (Homewood, Ill.: The Dorsey Press, Inc. and Richard D. Irwin, Inc., 1962). For the purposes of this text, the case study has been reorganized, shortened, updated, and extensively analyzed. All names are fictitious.

Third, this case study contains an unusually complete set of performance indices, which clearly supports the contention that the new leadership in Plant Y did not make people just *feel* more satisfied; it made them *perform* significantly better.

Fourth, the controlling "constants" in the situation made it possible to concentrate on the behavior of the new top manager and his role in the process of change. Specifically, it was found that during the entire period under the administration of the new manager:

1. The incumbents of offices in direct line of authority above the plant—division manager, group vice-president, operating executive vice-president, and corporation president—remained the same.
2. The plant itself operated with substantially the same supervisory personnel.
3. The formal structure of organization (number of levels, chain of command, span of control, and departmental functions) remained unchanged.
4. The plant continued to produce the same line of products under the same basic conditions of layout and technology.
5. Plant Y was subject to the same annual product changes and to external market conditions that other similar plants had to face.

That these factors remained constant throughout the process of change was fortunate. A change in one or more would have made it difficult if not impossible to account for the causes of change and, in particular, the role of the new top manager in the process.

Thus, in reading the case one should be aware that:

1. *Plant Y, under the former manager, had been in serious trouble. Not only was its performance poor, but expressions of bitter hostility and discouragement were heard at all levels of the organization.*
2. *In time, these expressions of hostility and discouragement virtually disappeared, and the plant as a production organization appeared to function more efficiently, not only by its own standards but also when compared with five other similar plants.*
3. *The change in attitudes and performance followed the introduction of a new manager.*

And, finally, although this case took place in a particular organizational setting in industry, the message it provides has been found to be applicable to many different types of organizational settings, whether they are business, education, family, government, hospital, military, religious, or voluntary.

As the prior discussion suggests, this case study of Plant Y could stand alone as interesting reading for a student of management or a management practitioner. And yet, if the Plant Y story were presented only in case format, it would have limited value. There is the danger that someone, after reading only the case, might want to generalize from this one situation and adopt the same change strategies in his own situation. We say danger because we realize that every situation is unique. What worked in Plant Y might not necessarily work in another setting. The key point is that effective managers or leaders are individuals who are able to diagnose their environment and determine the unique needs of their situation.[2] Edgar H. Schein expresses it well when he

---

[2]Research that supports the argument that there is no one "best" leadership style is readily available. As examples, see A. K. Korman," " 'Consideration,' 'Initiating Structure,' and Organizational Criteria—A Review," *Personnel Psychology: A Journal of Applied Research,* XIX, No. 4 (Winter 1966), 349–61, and Fred E. Fiedler, *A Theory of Leadership Effectiveness* (New York: McGraw-Hill Book Company, 1967).

THE PLANT Y CASE

contends that "the successful manager must be a good diagnostician and must value a spirit of inquiry. *If the abilities and motives of the people under him are so variable, he must have the sensitivity and diagnostic ability to be able to sense and appreciate the differences."*[3] *In other words, managers interested in change must be able to identify clues in their environment that suggest appropriate strategies to use* in that situation.

Recognizing the importance of diagnostic skills and not wanting to leave the practitioner frustrated by the conclusion that "it all depends on the situation," we attempt throughout this text to analyze and interpret the Plant Y story in terms of as many helpful behavioral science and systems theories and frameworks as possible.

Schein supports this attempt when he says, "Where we have erred is in oversimplifying and overgeneralizing. As empirical evidence mounts, it is becoming apparent that the frame of reference and value system which will help the manager most in utilizing people effectively is that of science and of systems theory."[4] *If managers examine these areas, they will test their assumptions about human nature and seek a better diagnosis. And if they do that, they will act more appropriately to whatever the demands of the situation are.*

Thus, the purposes for sharing the Plant Y story are twofold. First, we wanted practitioners to learn from a real life situation that effective change does not happen by chance. Second, we wanted practitioners to know that there are now available in the organizational behavior literature concepts and frameworks that can help them improve their diagnostic skills and develop appropriate change strategies, as well as understand why certain efforts to initiate change are effective and others are ineffective. To ac-

---

[3] Edgar H. Schein, *Organizational Psychology*, 2nd ed. (Englewood Cliffs, N.J.: Prentice-Hall, Inc., 1970), p. 70.
[4] Ibid., p. 71.

complish these two goals, the Plant Y story will be presented in a manner that is different from most case study presentations.

The remainder of this chapter will include two sections: The Organizational Structure of Plant Y and Frameworks for Analysis. The section on Plant Y will give some general background on the structure of this industrial assembly plant. The second section will touch upon general systems theory and provide a brief summary of concepts about motivation and leadership, which can be used in analyzing and interpreting the happenings in Plant Y. Beginning with Chapter 2, The Period of Disintegration, and continuing with Chapter 3, The Period of Change, Chapter 4, The Change Process in Retrospect—And the Results, and Chapter 5, The Epilogue, the case study of Plant Y will generally appear on the right-hand pages, with theoretical and analytical comments on the left-hand pages.

The case material from Plant Y was generated from extensive interviews with most of the managerial personnel involved during both the Period of Disintegration and the Period of Change. Interviews were conducted during these two time periods with foremen, general foremen, and members of top management, including the plant manager and members of his staff in the production and nonproduction departments. In addition to interviewing a sample of hourly workers, many hours of observation and informal discussions were spent in the plant's major production departments. Interviews were also conducted with the division manager (in charge of 6 assembly plants), his staff, the corporation vice-president over 8 divisions (22 plants) and the executive vice-president over the operations of 126 plants. Also interviewed were local and international union officers. Extensive background data on personnel and performance records were examined.

In presenting the case study material, information is set down with the least amount of interpretation consistent with orderly presentation. In most instances, the participants, members of the managerial group, "speak for themselves." It is recommended that, to maximize learning, the reader should first read section II in this chapter and then, starting with Chapter 2, read the case story on the right-hand page all the way through before looking at the theoretical comment or analysis on the left-hand page. (*In a few places, the case or the analysis may appear across both pages, as it does with the two sections in this chapter, The Organizational Structure of Plant Y and Frameworks of Analysis.*) *The authors urge this method because we feel that if a person first understands the basic story line and the critical incidents and then goes back to review the case with the theoretical and analytical comments, these interpretative materials take on more meaning. It will help the reader to see more clearly how theory can help to explain the success of this change effort. We feel that if, in the first reading, a person goes back and forth from the case to interpretation and then back to the case, much of the spirit and substance of the case itself might be lost.*

One may ask then why we did not separate the case and the interpretation completely. The reason we tried to keep them together facing each other on opposite pages was that we wanted to have any interpretation or analysis as close as possible to the case incident.

The format is different for the smaller Plant Z case. Beginning on page 172 the running story can be read straight through followed by the analytical section beginning on page 196. "Concluding Remarks" follow, beginning on p. 226.

The authors have not made a complete or comprehensive examination of all the behavioral science literature. Although we make no attempt to evaluate the theories and concepts presented, this is not to suggest that we accept them all as given. However, our purpose in this book is not to critique theories but rather to give the reader some feeling for the kinds of behavioral science theories and frameworks that are available and how they might be helpful to management practitioners and students as diagnostic tools.

The theories and frameworks presented include those of the authors as well as those of other leading behavioral science theorists and researchers.[5] Most of these theories and frameworks are covered in more detail in the fourth edition of the Hersey and Blanchard text, **Management of Organizational Behavior.** *That text may be useful as a companion to this book, but we hope that with the footnotes at the bottom of the analysis pages a person who becomes particularly interested in some concept or theory will have an easy and direct "road map" back into the literature. To further enhance that process, a theoretical summary of the condition of Plant Y is given at the end of the chapters describing the Period of Disintegration and The Epilogue.*

---

[5] The theories and concepts presented in this text do not obviously represent all the significant contributions in the field. The theories chosen are meant to be representative of the field and not all-inclusive. For more detail, see Paul Hersey and Kenneth H. Blanchard, *Management of Organizational Behavior*, 4th ed. (Englewood Cliffs, N.J.: Prentice-Hall, Inc., 1982).

II. THE ORGANIZATIONAL STRUCTURE
OF PLANT Y

Plant Y is one unit of a corporation comprised of more than a half million employees. At the top of the organizational pyramid is the board of directors, responsible primarily to the stockholders. The direct line organization down through the several levels to the lowest level of management at Plant Y is as follows:

	Chairman of the Board
	President
	Executive Vice-President
	Divisional Group Vice-President
	General Manager of the Division
	Plant Manager
Primary	Production Manager
Focus of Study	General Superintendent
PLANT Y	Department Superintendent
	General Foreman
	Foreman
	Hourly Wage Earners

The plant manager and the subordinate supervisory organization down through the foreman level are our primary concern. The division manager to whom the plant manager reports is also important. He is responsible for several final assembly plants located in different areas of the country.

The plant manager has ten department heads reporting to him, each in charge of certain functions generally comparable to those in any industrial plant. The plant manager's key subordinate is the production manager, who heads all of the operations directly connected with the assembly of the product. Reporting to him is a general superintendent. Under the general superintendent are five department superintendents, each running a general area of the plant. Each department superintendent has between one and four general foremen reporting to him. A general foreman might be in charge of one to six section foremen. Each section foreman has between fifteen and forty wage employees under him. In all, there are approximately twenty general foremen, just over one hundred foremen, and between two thousand to five thousand production workers, depending upon the rate of production and number of shifts.

Approximately one-third of the plant population is made up of persons in nonproduction groups. The title of the chief officers of each of these groups and the functions they head are: Resident Comptroller, Director of Personnel, Plant Engineer, Supervisor of Work Standards, Chief Inspector, Supervisor of Material and Production Control, Traffic Manager, Supervisor of Engineering Specifications, and Product Distributor.

Although the plant manager is held responsible for the final product, it should be noted that his actions and those of his subordinates are frequently circumscribed by policies, procedures, rules, orders, and reporting systems controlled at divisional and corporate levels. Despite these limitations, the corporation has a long-stated policy of "management decentralization."

As a high corporate official put it, "If a plant manager can consistently deliver the goods below a certain cost ceiling within an acceptable quality range, keep up his schedules, and not run afoul of corporation policy, then how he runs his own show is pretty much his own business."

In the total production flow, Plant Y, like its five sister plants spread around the United States, is the final operation in a series of highly synchronized operations, which begin at the ore pits and mines and carry through into basic manufacturing and the fabrication of several thousand parts in many other plants throughout the country. At a prescribed moment in time and space, these thousands of parts and units are brought to a focal point—the final assembly plant. There the many products of previous operations are fed into a maze of conveyors and machinery and emerge as completed products at a rate of more than 35 units per hour or more than 750 units a day on a two-shift basis. The retail value of **one day's production** is more than $2 million.

A striking feature of the overall operations at Plant Y is that many different types of the one product are assembled. Three distinct "makes" of the product are turned out, each make in many models and styles. Schedules are so contrived as to permit any product with any variety of specifications to be preceded or followed on the assembly line by a product of a completely different type with different specifications. The product must progress through the shop in a series of planned operations; the right part must arrive precisely in the right place at the right time. The product, through each production sequence, is delivered by the giant conveyor to and from the individual operators.

Operations are broken down into simple constituent components at the place of assembly. Thus, an assembly line is highly sensitive to any kind of change. A mechanical breakdown or an error in communication in the system can upset the work flow of the entire plant. A change in production schedule, and especially the annual model change, causes a realignment and reshuffling of literally thousands of work elements. Each breakdown or change sets in motion a whole series of actions within the organization from foreman to manager and higher. Operations as complex as these require an enormous amount of planning and coordination by the line organization and by specialized technical groups. (*If you are reading the case for the first time, skip to Chapter 2 and return to this section after reading the entire case.*)

III. FRAMEWORKS FOR ANALYSIS

A. General Systems Approach

In examining the happenings in Plant Y, a systems approach will be used. Huse and Bowditch define a system as "a series of interrelated and interdependent parts, such that the interaction or interplay of any of the subsystems (parts) affects the whole. In fact, if we use the systems approach, the interactions and interdependencies among the subsystems are at least as important as the individual components."[6]

An organization starts with *input* flows (people, energy, materials, or information) from *sources* in the external environment, which then get transformed by a technical and/or a human system into *outputs* or *outcomes*, which are provided to *users*. In addition, most systems include one or more self-regulating *feedback* mechanisms to guide and control the operation of the organization; that is, signals from the internal or external environment indicating that there is something wrong with the output that requires changes in the internal system or the inputs, or both.[7]

If the total system is healthy and functioning well, each of its parts or subsystems are effectively interacting with one another. Thus, an organization over a sustained period cannot afford to overemphasize the importance of productivity (outputs) at the expense of other parts of the total system and vice versa. At the

---

[6]E. Huse and J. Bowditch, *Behavior in Organization: A Systems Approach to Managing* (Reading, Mass.: Addison-Wesley, 1973), p. 28.

[7]Wendell L. French and Cecil H. Bell, Jr., *Organization Development: Behavioral Science Interventions for Organizational Improvement* (Englewood Cliffs, N.J.: Prentice-Hall, Inc., 1973), pp. 75–76.

same time, the internal management of the organization cannot ignore the needs of the external environment (the users).

B. Components of the Internal System

As the Plant Y story unfolds during its period of disintegration, the ineffective management and the broken linkages of the various components in the total system will become evident. As external economic conditions changed, the management of Plant Y responded by stressing outputs. It seemed to ignore the concerns of the internal human system. This, in turn, began to lead to the destruction of the total system.

Although one cannot overemphasize the effect external factors had on the increased emphasis on productivity, the major focus of the analysis of this case study will be on the internal system. Hersey and Scott identify four interrelated subsystems that comprise a complex organization such as Plant Y—an administrative/ structural system; a decision-making/information system; an economic/ technical system; a human/social system.[8] Each of these systems may be looked at abstractly as having distinguishable characteristics and as employing its own criteria of effectiveness.

---

[8]Much of the discussion on the components of the internal system was taken from lectures given by Dean Boris Yavitz, School of Business Administration, Columbia University. It was published as Paul Hersey and Douglas Scott, "A Systems Approach to Educational Organizations: Do We Manage or Administer?" *OCLEA,* pp. 3–5. There are many similar kinds of models with varying terminology and minor differences. As examples, see French and Bell, *Organization Development,* pp. 76–79; Daniel Katz and Robert L. Kahn, *The Social Psychology of Organization* (New York: John Wiley and Sons, Inc., 1966), p. 456; Harold J. Leavitt, "Applied Organizational Change in Industry: Structural, Technological and Humanistic Approaches," in *Handbook of Organizations,* ed. James G. March (Rand McNally and Co., 1965), pp. 114–45; John A. Seiler, *Systems Analysis in Organizational Behavior* (Homewood, Ill.: Richard D. Irwin, Inc., 1967), pp. 23–29; and E. L. Trist et al., *Organizational Choice* (London: Tavistock Publications, 1963).

1. Administrative/Structural Subsystem

This subsystem derives from Max Weber and other "classical" theorists who studied the structure of a bureaucracy.[9] Focus is on the authority and responsibility within the organization— "who does what for whom" and "who tells who(m) to do what, when, and why."

The description of the organization structure of Plant Y and its parent corporation given earlier depicts the administrative/ structural system. Although most of the elements of this system are fixed, the extent to which management decentralization exists in reality depends upon how smoothly operations are being run at the plant level. As implied, "management decentralization" exists for Plant Y "if the plant manager can consistently de-liver . . . ."

The criterion for effectiveness in this area is often the extent to which organizational "law and order" is maintained. For ex-ample, one could ask if in Plant Y corporate policies and practices are being clearly communicated to, accepted, and followed by its supervisory managers. Problems of managerial morale and motivation (part of the human/social subsystem) can result from the administrative/structural system if bureaucratic restraints cause those in managerial roles to have limited decision-making free-dom, to emphasize obedience to rules and regulations, and to be subject to close supervision in spite of the inherent skills and talent of the people performing these roles.

---

[9] Max Weber is known for the classic analysis of bureaucracy; see *The Theory of Social and Economic Organization,* trans. A. M. Henderson and ed. Talcott Parsons (New York: The Free Press of Glencoe, 1947) and *From Max Weber,* eds. Hans H. Gerth and C. Wright Mills (Oxford: Oxford University Press, 1946). See also R. L. Merton, et al., eds., *Reader in Bureaucracy* (Glencoe, Ill.: The Free Press, 1952).

2. Decision-Making/Information Subsystem

The decision-making/information subsystem focuses on decisions and informational flows to keep the system going. Summaries, reports, and projections of goals and priorities are basic. They provide managers with complete data on organizational operations so that various elements can be isolated, analyzed, monitored, and compared. Decisions on future plans and their implementation can be made. It was data from the decision-making or information system that alerted authorities to the fact that Plant Y was in trouble and something had to be done to stop the downward spiraling of productivity and morale.

Decision-making through the use of decision models or rules is also part of this system. Corporate and division headquarters establish the broad policy lines, while the lower echelon plant managers and supervisory personnel break the policy down into more detailed decisions. In such a system, general policy-making is concentrated at the top, policy specification carried out by the middle ranks, and detailed implementation of policy carried out by the lower ranks. The criterion for effectiveness in the decision-making/information system of an organization is the extent to which it is successful in adapting to changing environments, its internal environment, and the external environment, including the larger culture in which it is situated and operates.

3. Economic/Technical Subsystem

This subsystem focuses on how the work is to be done and the cost effectiveness of this work within the specific goals of the organization. In a manufacturing operation such as Plant Y, the focus is on the completion and distribution of the product within cost and quality specifications.

The concepts and ideas utilized in this subsystem include the division of labor or specialization, economy of operation, cost-benefit ratio, work flow design, and the machines and materials of the technology itself. The criteria for success for the economic/technical system are low cost and high quality. In the period of disintegration of Plant Y, the high direct and indirect cost and the low quality performance were further indicators that something drastic had to be done to stop this downward spiraling effect.

4. Human/Social Subsystem

This subsystem focuses on the motivation and needs of the members of the organization, and on the leadership provided or required. The major concern in this system is finding effective ways to develop continually the knowledge and skills that will contribute both to the development of its human resources and to the further achievement of organizational goals.

In terms of the development of human resources, managers of the human/social system might find Maslow's hierarchy of needs a useful framework.[10] According to Maslow, there seems to be a hierarchy into which human needs arrange themselves. The lowest level needs are *physiological*. These are the basic needs to sustain life itself—food, clothing, shelter. When these basic needs begin to be fulfilled, the next need level that people become concerned about is *safety* or *security* needs. These needs are essentially the need to be free of the fear of physical danger and deprivation of the basic physiological needs. Once physiological and safety needs are satisfied, *social* or *affiliation* needs will emerge as dominant in the need structure. People are social beings. They have a need to belong and to be accepted by others. After people begin to satisfy their need to belong, they generally want to be more than just a member of their group. They then feel the need

---

[10]Abraham H. Maslow, *Motivation and Personality* (New York: Harper and Row Publishers, 1954).

for *esteem*—both self-esteem and esteem from others. Once esteem needs are adequately satisfied, the *self-actualization* needs become most important. Self-actualization is a maximizing concept. That is, it is the need to maximize one's potential or the desire to become what one is capable of becoming. Until the lower level physiological and safety/security needs are fairly well satisfied, Maslow argues, social, esteem, and self-actualization needs will provide a person with little motivation.

Although Maslow is helpful in describing motives (needs, wants, and drives *within* an individual), Herzberg's Motivation-Hygiene Theory[11] is useful in suggesting the goals or incentives *outside* an individual that tend to satisfy his or her motives.[12] Herzberg found that when people felt dissatisfied with their jobs, they were concerned about the environment in which they were working or "hygiene or maintenance factors" (policies and administration, supervision, working conditions, interpersonal relations, wages, status, and job security). However, when people were satisfied with their jobs, they were motivated by the work itself, not by the environment. "Motivators" include opportunities for achievement, challenging work, increased responsibility, growth and development, and recognition for accomplishment. Herzberg found that if hygiene factors, just like Maslow's lower needs, are not fairly well satisfied, people will tend not to be interested in the challenge of a more responsible job and the resultant higher level need satisfaction.

Thus, Herzberg's Motivation-Hygiene Theory integrates well with Maslow's Hierarchy of Needs. In fact, it is helpful in suggesting the kinds of goals or incentives that managers can attempt

[11] Frederick Herzberg, Bernard Mausner, and Barbara Synderman, *The Motivation to Work* (New York: John Wiley and Sons, Inc., 1959), and Frederick Herzberg, *Work and the Nature of Man* (New York: World Publishing Co., 1966).

[12] For an extensive discussion of the difference between motives and goals and their effect on behavior, see Hersey and Blanchard, *Management of Organizational Behavior*, 4th ed., Chapter 2.

to provide to satisfy the various needs of their people. As examples, wages can help satisfy physiological needs; good working conditions and job security can help satisfy safety/security needs; the kind of policies and administration, supervision, and interpersonal relations can affect one's social need satisfaction; status and recognition for accomplishment can have an impact on esteem needs; and opportunities for achievement, challenging work, increased responsibility, and growth and development can help one maximize his or her potential and thus satisfy self-actualization needs on the job.

To motivate people effectively, management must use appropriate leadership styles in working with various people. A leadership theory that may be helpful to managers and leaders in diagnosing the demands of their situation has been developed by Hersey and Blanchard. Their theory, called "Situational Leadership Theory,"[13] will be used as an integrative framework throughout the analysis and interpretation of the Plant Y story. *This theory is based on a relationship between the amount of direction* (task behavior) *and the amount of socioemotional support* (relationship behavior) *leaders must provide and the level of task relevant "maturity" of their followers or group.* This is basically a leader-follower model, but one should not get the impression that these are the only situational variables that leaders must diagnose to determine appropriate leadership style. Effective leaders must also consider such other factors as the style and expectations of their boss, their associates (peers), and the organization, as well as job demands and time.

According to Situational Leadership Theory, *task behavior* is the extent to which a leader engages in one-way communication by explaining what each subordinate is to do as well as

---

[13] "Situational Leadership Theory" was developed at the Center for Leadership Studies, Ohio University, Athens, Ohio. The essence of the theory was first published in Hersey and Blanchard, "Life Cycle Theory of Leadership," *Training and Development Journal,* May 1969. For the latest modification and clarification, see Hersey and Blanchard, *Management of Organizational Behavior,* 4th ed., Chapter 7.

when, where, and how tasks are to be accomplished. *Relationship behavior* is the extent to which a leader engages in two-way communication by providing socioemotional support, "psychological strokes," and facilitating behaviors. *Maturity* is defined in Situational Leadership Theory as the capacity to set high but attainable goals (achievement-motivation[14]), willingness and ability to take responsibility, and education and/or experience of an individual or a group. *These variables of maturity should be considered only in relation to a specific task to be performed.* That is to say, an individual or a group is not mature or immature in any *total* sense. People tend to have varying degrees of maturity depending on the specific task, function, or objective that a leader is attempting to accomplish through their efforts.

According to Situational Leadership Theory, there are four different maturity levels that may describe people in terms of accomplishing a specific task, all of which require a different leadership style.

1. *Low Follower Maturity.* At this maturity level, people tend to lack both motivation ("willingness") and competence ("ability") to do a particular task. Thus, the leadership style with the highest probability of success in this situation would be high task/low relationship behavior; that is, leaders working with people at this maturity level must define their role and direct them as to what, how, when, and where to do the task. This is sometimes called the "telling" style.

2. *Low to Moderate Follower Maturity.* At this maturity level, people tend to have the motivation to do a particular task but lack the ability. Thus, the leadership style that appears to be most appropriate to this situation

---

[14] David McClelland, et al., *The Achievement Motive* (New York: Appleton-Century-Crofts, 1953), and *The Achieving Society* (Princeton, N.J.: D. Van Nostrand Co., Inc., 1961).

would be high task/high relationship behavior; that is, leaders working with people at this maturity level must still provide most of the direction (because of the follower(s) lack of ability in the area), but now can attempt through two-way communication and socioemotional support (because of the demonstrated motivation) to get the follower(s) to accept decisions that have to be made and the directions that must be given. This is sometimes called the "selling" style.

3. *Moderate to High Follower Maturity*. At this maturity level, people tend to have the ability to do a particular task but seem to lack the motivation. The initial leadership style that tends to be most effective in this situation would be high relationship/low task behavior; that is, leaders working with people at this maturity level need not provide much initial direction (because of the follower(s) ability in the area) but should share in decision-making through two-way communication, thus facilitating behavior that will release the blocked motivation. This is sometimes called the "participating" style.

4. *High Follower Maturity*. At this maturity level, people tend to have both the motivation and ability to do a particular task. The leadership style with the highest probability of success in this situation would be low relationship/low task behavior; that is, leaders working with people at this maturity level demonstrate their confidence and trust in them by providing opportunities for them to "run their own show." This is sometimes called the "delegating" style.

In examining the human/social system in Plant Y, Situational Leadership Theory will be used as an integrative framework for analyzing the success of that subsystem, as well as linking it to other subsystems (economic/technical, administrative/structural, and so on).

C. Dynamics within a System

Management involves working with and through individuals and groups to accomplish organizational goals.[15] Although more emphasis in the analysis of Plant Y will be placed on examining the human/social system than on any of the other subsystems, it should be emphasized that within a systems approach there is a clear understanding that changes in one subsystem effect changes in all parts of the total system. Thus, one may concentrate on the human/social system, buy not without considering events that occur in the other subsystems. Guest[16] emphasized this point in his original presentation of the Plant Y story by stressing the simultaneous interaction of the *social* and *technical* dimensions of organizational reality:

> *On his part the social scientist often makes the error of concentrating on human motivation and group behavior without fully accounting for the technical environment which circumscribes, even determines, the roles which the actors play. Motivation, group structure, interaction processes, authority— none of these abstractions of behavior takes place in a technological vacuum.*

As will become clear in the Plant Y story, both social and technical malfunctions combined to cause the initial downward spiraling of performance. Later changes in both these systems made the eventual improvements possible. The pioneer work on the reciprocity of human resources and technology by Trist and Emery[17] at Tavistock Institute of Human Relations in England;

---

[15] Hersey and Blanchard, *Management of Organizational Behavior,* 4th ed., Chapter 5.

[16] Guest, *Organizational Change,* p. 4.

[17] See E. L. Trist and K. W. Banford, "Some Social and Psychological Consequences of the Long Wall Method of Coal Getting," *Human Relations,* 4, No. 1 (1951), 3–38, and F. E. Emery, "Some Characteristics of Socio-Technical Systems," Doc. No. 527, *The Tavistock Institute of Human Relations,* January 1959. More recent work includes Trist, et al., *Organizational Choice* (London: Tavistock, 1963), and Emery and Trist, "The Causal Texture of Organizational Environments," *Human Relations,* 18 (1965), 21–31.

Guest, Walker and Turner at the Yale Technology Project; and the amplification by Thorsrud[18] of the Work Research Institute in Oslo, Norway, led Guest to conclude that "a basic unit of organization in our society, the factory, is best described not as a social system alone nor as a technical system but as a socio-technical system."[19] As the Plant Y story unfolds, one will quickly become aware of the significance of linking both dimensions and the impact that changes in one has on the other.

---

[18] Einar Thorsrud, although not widely published, has long been recognized as a leader in the field.

[19] Guest, *Organizational Change*, p. 135.

chapter
2

Period of
Disintegration

ANALYSIS

These changes illustrate the effect that external factors such as market conditions (which are beyond the control of the organization) can have on the internal function of the system.

Arnseberg, Chapple, Homans, Richardson[1] and other members of the interactionist school have developed a methodology for examining the ongoing interactions of people in an organization. As used here, the term "interaction" describes an occurrence involving two or more people in which the actions of one person stimulate a reaction by another (or others). In examining the interaction patterns in an organization, people in this field observe the direction, frequency, and duration of interpersonal contacts.

With the change in the market conditions, one can see a pattern beginning of frequent interactions originating down from corporate headquarters. The frequency of top-down initiated interactions made everyone feel that the "pressure was on." It will be interesting to observe how this pattern of direction, frequency, and duration will spread throughout all supervisory levels of Plant Y during this disintegration period.

---

[1]Conrad M. Arensberg, "Behavior and Organization: Industrial Studies," in *Social Psychology at the Crossroads,* eds. John H. Rohrer and Muzafer Sherif. (New York: Harper and Brothers, 1951); Elliot D. Chapple and Carleton Coon, *Principles of Anthropology* (New York: Henry Holt and Company, Inc., 1942); George C. Homans, *The Human Group* (New York: Harcourt, Brace, and Company, 1950); Frederick L. W. Richardson and Charles R. Walker, *Human Relations in An Expanding Company* (New Haven: Labor and Management Center, Yale University, 1948); and William F. Whyte, "Framework for the Analysis of Industrial Relations," *Industrial and Labor Relations Review,* Vol. 3, No. 3 (April 1950).

I. PLANT Y RELATIONSHIP TO THE DIVISION

At the beginning of this study the market conditions in the industry were changing. Production schedules had to be substantially altered. Although all six final assembly plants of the corporation faced similar conditions, the effects on Plant Y were extremely critical. Production costs, including direct and indirect labor costs, were increasing at a much higher rate when compared with other plants. Quality and inspection indicators showed marked deterioration. Labor grievances were skyrocketing. Absenteeism and turnover were increasing. Obviously something was going wrong. Corporate and division officials were becoming deeply concerned as they compared Plant Y's record with the other plants.

The staff at Plant Y was acutely aware of the situation. They, too, received the periodic reports comparing all the plants. They also observed the increasing communications originating at division and corporate levels and directed at the Plant Y manager in the form of demands for improved performance. Urgent telephone calls, telex messages, letters, and memoranda were stepped up. Higher officials were making more frequent visits to Plant Y than to any of the other plants. Divisional staff members representing accounting, quality control, material control, personnel, and other functions were in frequent touch with their subordinate counterparts in the plant and with the manager himself. Dealers of the product were complaining about poor delivery dates and alleged quality defects. The various divisions whose products were being assembled at Plant Y were communicating almost every day with the manager and his staff, either directly or through division officials. "Pressure" was a common expression heard at all levels.

Katz identified three important managerial skills—**technical** *(for the performance of a specific task[s])*, **human** *(working with and through other people)*, *and* **conceptual** *(seeing where everything fits into the total organization).*[2] *It is possible that Stewart, having been in staff positions with relatively few subordinates, relied mostly on his technical skills. Upon taking over a very large organization, he may not have been able to respond effectively in terms of his human and conceptual skills.*

In his work in human organizations, Likert identifies three variables—causal, intervening, and end result—that may be used to examine the effectiveness of an organization.[3]

Causal *variables are those factors that influence the course of development within an organization and its results or accomplishments (management style and strategies, organizational structure and objectives, technology, and others). These are the independent variables that can be changed by the organization and its management, not variables that are beyond its control, such as business conditions.*

Leadership strategies, skills, behavior, and other causal variables affect the human resources or **intervening** *variables in an organization. According to Likert, intervening variables represent the current condition of the internal state of the organization and are reflected in its skills, loyalty, commitment to objectives, motivations, problem solving, decision making, climate and capacity for effective interaction.*

Output or end-result *variables are the dependent variables that reflect the achievements of the organization.*

Intervening variables are produced largely by the causal variables and, in turn, have influence upon the end-result variables. The "slip-

---

[2] These descriptions were adapted from a classification developed by Robert L. Katz, "Skills of an Effective Administrator," *Harvard Business Review*, January–February 1955, pp. 33–42.

[3] Rensis Likert, *The Human Organization* (New York: McGraw-Hill Book Company, 1969), pp. 26–29.

THE PLANT Y CASE

George Stewart (as stated earlier, all names are fictitious), the manager at the present time, knew that he was, as he put it, "on the spot." He had been appointed manager three years earlier, having had an outstanding record for his previous technical competence, mostly in staff positions. Plant Y, when he took over, had been "in the middle of the pack" in its performance record, not the best nor the poorest. Indications of "slippage" began about a year and a half after Stewart took over.

page" that occurred after Stewart took over would be an indicator, in Likert terms, that the plant manager was possibly an important causal variable, which was a negative stimulus on the human organization (intervening variables) and thus resulting in a low productivity (end-result variables) response.

Here we are beginning to see the initial stages of the "pecking order" concept. The management of one level of an organization receives pressure from the level above. They put pressure on the level below them, and so on down the line to all the supervisory levels of the organization. With this pecking order phenomenon comes similar high frequency top-down, short-duration crisis interactions. As Homans[4] suggests, where all interactions are unilateral, "negative sentiments" will tend to result.

Lewin frequently observed that when an individual fails to meet the performance expectations of others, there is a strong tendency for that individual to project blame outward in an effort to preserve some measure of self-esteem.[5]

Guest postulates that as the superior-directed interactions increase, the ability of the subordinate to initiate upward communications, **at least as perceived by the subordinate,** *decreases.[6]*

Thompson describes this as "bureaupathic" behavior, a result of growing insecurity about one's authority. The "leader" feels that the legitimacy of his authority is in danger.[7]

[4] Homans, *The Human Group.*

[5] Kurt Lewin, "Psychology of Success and Failure," *Occupations,* 14 (June 1936), 926–30.

[6] Robert H. Guest, *Organizational Change: The Effect of Successful Leadership* (Homewood, Ill.: The Dorsey Press, Inc. and Richard D. Irwin, Inc., 1962), Chapter 6.

[7] Victor A. Thompson, *Modern Organization* (New York: Alfred A. Knopf, Inc., 1961), Chapter 8.

THE PLANT Y CASE

II. THE PLANT MANAGER'S ROLE
IN THE PROCESS OF DISINTEGRATION

To his subordinates, carrying out directives from the division manager appeared to be the chief preoccupation of the plant manager. On at least two occasions Stewart made recordings of his staff meetings and played them back to the division manager. A member of the plant staff observed later: "He was trying to show the division manager that he was carrying out orders. I think he was also trying to put the blame on his own staff. They knew this."

Stewart himself explained his own position during the crisis period:

> They just don't know in the central office what he have to face. They don't know how to get down to our level. They think everything can be done by a schedule, no matter how fantastic. They keep saying to me, "Why can't you do it? So-and-so in another plant can." Then when so-and-so has the same problem, they shift to another so-and-so. This competition thing can be carried too far. When I get this kind of pressure on me, I've always been able to roll with the punches, but now I get butterflies in my stomach. It makes it hard for me. I can't tell those below me that I can't do anything about this impossible schedule, so, of course, I get blamed for a lot of it. I can't treat my superintendents the way I get treated. They would just pack up and go home.

ANALYSIS

Etzioni[8] *discusses the differences between* **position** *power and* **personal** *power. His distinction springs from his concept of power as the ability to induce or influence behavior. He claims that power is derived from an organizational office, personal influence, or both. Individuals who are able to induce another individual to do a certain job because of their* position *are considered to have* **position power;** *individuals who derive their power from their followers are considered to have* **personal power.** *Stewart does not seem to have developed any* **personal** *power with his people.*

In recent years the notion of **power** *has been made more specific. French and Raven describe five bases of power.*[9] *They include* **coercive** *power (use of punishment),* **legitimate** *power (similar to Etzioni's position power),* **expert** *power (skill, knowledge, and expertise),* **reward** *power (pay and recognition), and* **referent** *power (similar to Etzioni's "personal" power). Raven and Kruglanski later added* **information** *power, in which a person has special access to critical information important to a group or organization.*[10] *Hersey and Goldsmith observed another source of power which they called* **connection** *power, derived from the leader's special connections with important persons other than followers.*[11] *Stewart in the Plant Y case made use of some of these power bases, but the subordinate perceptions were that he relied almost exclusively on* **coercive** *power.*

Hersey and Blanchard emphasize that there is a difference between self-perception and the perception of others (style). Leadership style is not how leaders think they behave in a situation but how others (most importantly, their followers) perceive their behavior. This is often a difficult concept for leaders to understand. And yet, it should be remembered

---

[8]Amatai Etzioni, *A Comparative Analysis of Complex Organizations* (New York: The Free Press, 1961).

[9]J. R. P. French and B. H. Raven, "The Social Bases of Power," in D. Cartwright, *Studies in Social Power* (Ann Arbor: University of Michigan, Institute for Social Research, 1959).

[10]B. H. Raven and W. Kruglanski, "Conflict and Power," in P. G. Swingle, ed., *The Structure of Conflict* (New York: Academic Press, 1975), pp. 177–219.

[11]Hersey and Blanchard, *Management of Organizational Behavior*, 4th ed., p. 178.

I can't say these things to my people. I can't say them to my superiors. Results are all that matter to them. I wish I had some way of getting this up to the top where it might do some good. It comes from the very top of the corporation. I would get hung if I said this higher up.

We have a labor turnover right now hitting close to sixty men a day. Still they call me up from central headquarters and ask me why I'm not on schedule.

Stewart rationalized that things were not going well by saying:

The new men we got are no good. Just yesterday I jumped a man who was not on his job. I asked where he was going and if he had asked permission. It's impossible for me alone to keep everybody in line, but I do the best I can.

The plant manager's comments and those of others show a distinct pattern, as well as a curious inconsistency. To Stewart the pattern of communications was characterized by the constant use of orders and threats by the division; he no longer felt that he had the "power" to respond effectively; his role was primarily defensive. He felt that he was the victim of conditions—the "impossible" production schedule over which he had no control. The division policy of encouraging interplant competition, a policy generally accepted by the other plant managers, was not considered legitimate by Stewart, at least in the way it was being used on him by the division.

The inconsistency in Stewart's comments is that he indicated reluctance to deal with subordinates the way the division was dealing with him, yet a few moments later he described how he "jumped a man" and tried "to keep everybody in line." He *that people whom a leader is attempting to influence will respond to* **their** *perception of reality, not the leader's perception. Thus, while Stewart felt that he was a good "buffer" with top management and was not transferring pressure below, his subordinates undoubtedly saw him the same way he saw his superiors—putting pressure on with no questions asked (high task/low relationship behavior). This difference in perception could have been valuable information for Stewart and could have helped him to understand why everyone was avoiding him and not giving him "straight answers" (as we will see). Yet, this kind of information is not easy to obtain. People are often reluctant to level with one another about how the other person is coming across, especially if they are in a superior-subordinate relationship.*

McGregor[12] suggested that there are two different sets of assumptions about human nature and human motivation. One set of assumptions, which he called Theory X, suggests that people are basically lazy, unreliable, irresponsible, motivated only by Maslow's lower level physiological and safety needs, and, therefore, the only way one gets anything out of them in a work situation is to direct, control, and closely supervise their behavior. Theory Y assumptions, on the other hand, reflect a more positive view of people; they could be creative and self-directed at work if properly motivated at the higher social, esteem, and self-actualization need levels, as described by Maslow.

Argyris[13] identifies behavior Patterns A and B to correspond with Theory X and Theory Y. Pattern A represents leader behavior characterized by close supervision, a high degree of structure, and "telling" behavior; Pattern B, according to Argyris, is characterized by general supervision, high consideration, and "participating" behavior. As Argyris emphasizes, "although XA and YB are **usually** *associated with each other*

---

[12] Douglas McGregor, *The Human Side of Enterprise* (New York: McGraw-Hill Book Company, 1960).

[13] Chris Argyris, *Management and Organizational Developments: The Path From XA to YB* (New York: McGraw-Hill Book Company, 1971).

appeared to denounce interplant competition himself, but his subordinates accused him of encouraging the same kind of interpersonal and interdepartmental rivalry.

In addition to providing written directives, Stewart met with members of his staff individually and as a group. Staff meetings were held sometimes once a week, but they were not scheduled on a regular basis. They were called as a direct result of some new directive or complaint from the division or as a result of some emergency situation in the plant. In content the meetings focused on short-run solutions to immediate production problems. Few were directed at what the members called "long-range planning." In the meetings Stewart generally directed remarks to one or another individual; he would request information on a given problem or ask for an explanation; he frequently interrupted the members, they reported, with his own opinion or orders; there were few lateral discussions among members of the staff. A department head observed:

> *We spent most of our time making explanations about why something went wrong and who made it go wrong. Each one tried to cover up for his own department, trying to prove he was carrying out orders, like Mr. Stewart said we should. We all recognized that the squeeze was on the manager from above, but he didn't have to hammer away with orders to get this done or that done, when no single one of us could do much about it.*

in everyday life, they do not have to be. Under certain circumstances, Pattern A could go with Theory Y or Pattern B with Theory X."[14]

Stewart's comments as well as the observations of other managers suggest that he was an XA manager—that is, he seemed to have negative assumptions about people and behaved in controlling, structured ways. He emphasized, in Likert's terms, output variables without taking into consideration the deteriorating condition of the human resources (intervening variables). As a result, the pressure from the top was being transferred throughout the entire organization.

Two points about assumptions that are worth noting. First of all, Hersey and Blanchard argue that having low expectations (Theory X assumptions) for the performance of individuals can become a self-fulfilling prophecy. This occurs when individuals are always treated as if they are lazy and unreliable, and, thus, are always told what to do and how to do it, with little consideration expressed for their ideas or feelings. If they are treated that way long enough, after a while they begin to behave as if they were that kind of person. This can become a downward spiraling effect. Low expectations result in low performance, which reinforces the low expectations and produces even lower productivity. This self-fulfilling prophecy seemed to be occurring in Plant Y under Stewart.

Second, Argyris compares bureaucratic/pyramidal values (the organizational counterpart to Theory X assumptions about people), which still dominate most organizations, with a more humanistic/democratic value system (the organizational counterpart to Theory Y assumptions about people).

---

[14] Ibid., p. 12.

Most events involving Stewart and single members of the line organization assumed essentially the same pattern—giving orders and directives to individuals, regardless of the effects of such orders on other individuals or groups. The plant manager's frequent trips to the production departments were usually in direct response to an emergency condition, such as a line breakdown, a report of continued quality trouble, or a stoppage in the material flow to operating stations. Stewart asked questions and gave direct orders. As one general foreman put it: "He has the first and last word. I just say 'Yes, sir.' "

This is further evidence that, in Plant Y, attempts to influence people's behavior is done only through the use of position power—sanctions, punishment, deprivation of rewards, and such. There was little attempt by Stewart or any of the supervisory managers to gain some personal power from the people who worked for them. This is particularly evident when one realizes that efforts to bolster the productivity of Plant Y were done by coercive change methods. According to Hersey and Blanchard,[15] coercive change begins when someone with position power imposes some change on a group or organization, which, through the use of punishment and negative reinforcement, forces people to behave in new ways. Since Stewart was under tremendous pressure to "turn things around" with all due haste, the speed advantage of this change cycle might have motivated him to use these coercive methods.

Although this method is fast, it necessitates close, direct supervision, which can destroy any personal power accumulated at lower supervisory levels. A disadvantage of using position power to influence people

---

[15] Hersey and Blanchard, *Management of Organizational Behavior*, 4th ed., Chapter 10.

III. VERTICAL RELATIONSHIPS
BELOW THE PLANT MANAGER

The superintendents perceived the manager's behavior in much the same way that Stewart himself perceived the behavior of *his* superiors. Motivated to act out of fear for their jobs, not by the belief that the orders would satisfy their needs or solve technical problems, they chose the only alternative—follow orders. One superintendent summed it up:

> *This plant is a one-man show, so people are not taught to be self-reliant. Fear, that's the trouble. Nobody questions an order. If the boss said 'Break a window,' most of the fellows would do just that. In the meetings we have they just give us hell. Nothing constructive is ever done.*

Although the general foremen were still further removed from the manager in the "chain of command," their perception of Stewart's behavior was essentially the same. Obedience to orders, enforcement of rules, the exercise of power through threat of punishment, failure to listen—these were the chief characteristics of Stewart's behavior as seen by general foremen:

> *The top people are too quick to condemn, and they never compliment the men for a good job. They tell us it is good human relations to do it, but they don't do it themselves. The only time I have anything to do with the manager is when he comes down and chews me out, usually in front of the others. I expect to be called on the carpet for the mistakes I make, but*

is that it tends to be volatile. It can lead to animosity and hostility, particularly if the people being coerced see themselves as more mature than the high task/low relationship style ("telling") that is being used on them assumes. If that happens, a manager should take heed of the warning of Machiavelli,[16] namely, that the continuous use of fear (position power) leads to hatred. Hatred often results in overt and covert attempts to undermine and overthrow.

Here is another example of Argyris's "decreased interpersonal competence"[17] because of too much emphasis on impersonal bureaucratic values. The "tragedy" here is that Stewart himself may have felt locked in to such a value system. Recall his earlier words, "I can't treat my superintendents the way I get treated."

One of the basic principles of organizational design proclaimed by Fayol[18] and other classical theorists[19] of the early 1900s is **chain of command.** *This principle states that everyone from the bottom to the top should have a superior to whom he or she is accountable. "From experience, military, governmental, religious, and economic organizations have discovered the value of an unbroken chain of command leading*

---

[16] Nicollò Machiavelli, "Cruelty and Clemency and Whether It Is Better to Be Loved or Feared," *The Prince* (Northbrook, Ill.: AHM Publishing Corporation, 1947), Chapter XVII, pp. 47–50.

[17] Argyris, "Interpersonal Barriers," and *Interpersonal Competence.*

[18] Henri Fayol, *Industrial and General Administration* (Paris: Dunod, 1925).

[19] See J. O. Mooney and A. C. Reiley, *Onward Industry* (New York: Harper and Brothers, 1931); Luther Gulich and Lyndall F. Urwick, eds., *Papers on the Science of Administration* (New York: Columbia University Press, 1937); and Lyndal F. Urwick, *The Theory of Organization* (New York: American Management Association, 1952).

this should be done by my own boss. The trouble with this plant is that those at the top are doing most of the chewing out directly. On the second shift, I get less of this just from the simple fact that the top people are not around as much. But this is no way to run a plant. If you have an organization and it spells out who is to order who around, then they should use it. I go to the men directly but only to look at the workers' problem. I don't bawl them out.

The foremen saw considerably less of the plant manager than did those at higher levels. However, their comments only echoed those of the general foremen and superintendents.

Stewart would come down and stand next to me and point out some man and say, "What the hell is that guy doing?" I get all nervous and confused and I suppose I'm expected to do something about it. The man may have a perfectly good excuse, but I have to pretend to straighten it out then and there. That doesn't make it any easier for the foreman with his men. You can't work under a manager like that.

It was not uncommon for members of higher levels in supervision to ignore the chain of command and to initiate contacts directly with those some levels below. As one superintendent observed:

I came from another plant as department superintendent. First thing that struck me here was that they were not paying any attention to the line organization. There's too much of the superintendent giving orders directly to the foreman and bypassing the general foreman.

from the lowest level private, citizen, parishioner, or worker to the most elevated general, president, bishop, or executive."[20]

In Plant Y there was a clear chain of command from the plant manager to department heads to department superintendents to general foremen to foremen. What was happening was that Stewart and other supervisory managers were "short-circuiting" the chain of command and sometimes dealing with people who were two or more levels below them on the hierarchy. This practice not only confused the communication networks, but made managers at every level insecure (in Maslow's terms) because they no longer knew clearly where they stood with their boss or in the organization itself. It also undermined any personal power that a manager had with his subordinates. As Hersey and Blanchard[21] claim, personal power and position power are dependent variables. That is, often the perception of one's personal power depends on one's clout (position power) with his or her superior; yet all this short-circuiting destroyed any perception that subordinates may have had about their boss' "clout upstairs."

Kelman[22] discusses three mechanisms or processes for changing the attitudes or behavior of people: compliance, identification, and internalization. **Compliance** occurs when an individual is forced to change by the direct manipulation of rewards and punishment by someone in a power position. In this case, behavior appears to have changed when the change agent is present but is often dropped when supervision is removed. **Identification** occurs when one or more models are provided in the environment, models from whom an individual can learn new behavior patterns by identifying with them and trying to become like them. **Internalization** occurs when individuals are placed in a situation where new behaviors are demanded of them if they are to operate successfully

---

[20] Ross A. Webber, *Management: Basic Elements of Managing Organizations* (Homewood, Ill.: Richard D. Irwin, Inc., 1975), p. 387.

[21] Hersey and Blanchard, *Management of Organizational Behavior*, 4th ed., Chapter 5.

[22] H. C. Kelman, "Compliance, Identification, and Internalization: Three Processes of Attitude Change," *Conflict Resolution*, II (1958), 51–60.

The Plant Y Case

General foremen and superintendents were disciplining workers directly. One foreman expressed it this way:

I get aggravated by the interference from the general foreman and the superintendent. They are always trying to run the men in my section. Today the general foreman stopped a man on the line and told him off. I heard about it later. This has happened before, and I've seen one of my men quit on the spot. I resent this. I feel I should have a chance to try things my way first. This interference weakens my position with the men. The men get to wonder who is their boss, and I don't blame them.

Lack of time to exchange information, fear of the consequences of not obeying orders, and doubts about the legitimacy of orders were often cited as sources of friction between a subordinate and his boss. The foreman was caught in the middle. Subject to punishment from above if he failed to carry out orders, he risked alienating his men if he obeyed orders as given. Like those above him, he had no mechanism of appeal (his workers had a mechanism—the union). And recall the comment of Stewart himself: "I can't say these things to my people. I can't say them to my superiors."

in that situation. They learn these new behavior patterns not only because they are necessary to survive but because of need changes induced by coping with the new situation.

In Plant Y, lower level managers were initially in an environment where they could treat their people the way they wanted to be treated. For some managers, this behavior had probably even been internalized. But at present with the "pressure on," they are forced through compliance to identify with the high task/low relationship ("telling") style of Stewart and the managers above them. Gradually, this behavior is starting to be internalized as the needs of these managers begin to change to survival as the coercive identification models remain active in the organization.

It is useful to examine the behavior of these lower level managers in terms of behavior Patterns A and B (Argyris[23]) and Theory X and Theory Y (McGregor[24]).

Comments by some of the managers suggest that they may be YA managers at this time. In Argyris's terms they have positive assumptions about people but because of the top-down pressure they are behaving in directive, controlling ways. If managers are forced to behave in authoritarian ways long enough, this initial discrepancy between their attitude and behavior may cease and they might begin to take on Theory X attitudes, too. This is particularly possible if their subordinates respond to their Pattern A behavior in immature, irresponsible ways and performance suffers.

[23] Argyris, *Management and Organizational Development.*
[24] McGregor, *The Human Side of Enterprise.*

The dilemma of how a supervisor wanted to behave toward subordinates and how he felt he had to behave was in many instances sharply expressed by the new foremen, many of whom had been promoted from the ranks. They continued to accept, for a while at least, norms of behavior that hourly workers thought were legitimate. One foreman remarked about the transition to the behavior described above:

> When I used to be a man on the line, I knew the way I'd like to be treated. When I got to be foreman, I started to treat my men in the same way . . . but you just can't do that. You can't change overnight what's been going on for years. Now I treat my men the way they have been treated more or less in the past. If a man is habitually late . . . I just turn him in, that's all. They can always quit if they don't like the job.

A major difference between task behavior and relationship behavior is whether there is one-way or two-way communication occurring.[25] Task behavior involves one-way communication—the leader "tells" the subordinate(s) what, when, where, and how to do something. On the other hand, relationship behavior consists of two-way or multiway communication between leader and follower(s). In Plant Y everything was "telling" from the top down, with little communication going back up through the chain of command or horizontally to other departments.

What is happening here is that technical problems (which could be solved if there was, in Argyris's terms,[26] some "interpersonal competence" in the organization) are now magnifying problems in the human system. Security and safety needs (Maslow[27]) are becoming dominant among all involved.

Here is a classic example of the dysfunctional use of administrative control mechanisms as described by Guest.[28] The quality control mechanism is being used here arbitrarily and as a punitive device. The result is a negative emotional response, which is subverting the very purpose of the mechanism itself, namely, good quality.

---

[25] Hersey and Blanchard, *Management of Organizational Behavior,* 4th ed., Chapter 4.
[26] Argyris, "Interpersonal Barriers," and *Interpersonal Competence.*
[27] Maslow, *Motivation and Personality.*
[28] Guest, *Organizational Change,* Chapter 5.

CASE

In a hierarchical organization, it is axiomatic that information and orders are generally transmitted through the chain of command from superior to subordinate. It is assumed, also, that the upward flow of communications generally takes place in reverse through these same channels. Supervisors at middle and lower levels reported that the overwhelming number of contacts involved the issuance of orders by superiors resulting from immediate technical and organizational emergencies. Very little information or advice was filtered up the line.

Varying degrees of antagonism and fear (of subordinates about superiors) characterized the comments. One general foreman stated it this way:

> *Take like on this scheduling problem I'm having. The line today is all out of balance, and the heavy jobs are bunching through all at once. We can't keep to the schedule, and our quality is shot to hell. Some of us know what the trouble is, but does my boss or the fellows in the front office come down to get our opinion of what's wrong? Hell, no. The boss comes up to me today and throws a standard quality report in my face. So I have to do something. He outranks me, so I have to go through the motions of telling my foremen to straighten it out. The trouble here is that there is too much of this superiority in rank. This prevents people from getting right down to brass tacks and finding out what the real trouble is.*

Here the foreman is recognizing his boss' expertise (technical skill), but suggests he is not using this knowledge to solve problems. At the same time any skills his boss may have had in working with people (human skills) are being suppressed by the top-down pressure and his subsequent increasing security needs. However, if this top-down punitive management approach is to be stopped, lower level managers like this foreman must begin to take a stand and try to influence "up." When that attempt occurs, the foreman would become the "potential leader" and his boss would be the "potential follower."[29] *Such a reversal in the normal direction of leadership flow is difficult to accomplish in an organization like Plant Y where top managers are undermining job security and relying only on position power to influence subordinates.*

This illustrates the interrelationship between all the subsystems in the organization. Problems in the economic/technical system negatively affect the interactions in the human/social system, which in turn distort communication in the information/decision-making system and the administrative/structural system.[30]

---

[29] Hersey and Blanchard argue that when thinking about Situational Leadership Theory, one should not think of leader-follower relationships as only hierarchical. Any time a person attempts to influence the behavior of another individual, even one's boss, that person is the "potential leader" and the individual he or she is attempting to influence is the "potential follower." See *Management of Organizational Behavior*, 4th ed., Chapters 4 and 7.

[30] These components of the internal system were taken from Paul Hersey and Douglas Scott, "A Systems Approach to Educational Organizations: Do We Manage or Administer?" *OCLEA*, pp. 3–5.

The same incident on the same day was described by a foreman under this same general foreman:

> *My boss is sharp and he knows how this scheduling business raises the devil in my section, but he is under a helluva lot of pressure. He's just as scared of his job as we are. He comes over and tells me to get my quality in better shape. It's one thing to issue an order; that's the easy way out. It's quite something else to carry it out when you can't control what causes the trouble.*

IV. LINE-STAFF RELATIONSHIPS

Progressive assembly operations require close coordination between the activities of the operating (line) groups and those of the nonproduction (staff) departments. The latter would include material and production control, inspection, work standards, and comptroller.

Material and Production Control

Bottlenecks and shortages were becoming chronic. In some respects the problem was a technical matter; the system of material flow and the layout of equipment were inadequate in some areas. As the technical difficulties worsened, interpersonal conflicts increased. These conflicts in turn created further technical difficulties.

A general foreman described a typical sequence of events stemming from a material holdup:

ANALYSIS

This is a typical example of Guest's sociotechnical cycle theory showing how purely technical problems result in negative human confrontations and in turn make it difficult to solve the technical problems rationally.[31]

According to Blake, Shepard, and Mouton,[32] *there are three attitudinal sets that people can have toward conflict: (1) conflict is inevitable, agreement is impossible; (2) conflict is not inevitable, yet agreement is impossible; and (3) although there is conflict, agreement is possible. These attitudinal sets will lead to predictable behavior depending upon the way the people involved see the "stakes," that is, the extent to which they see that the conflict is important or having value. If people think conflict is inevitable, agreement is impossible, their behavior will range from being passive to very active. When the stakes are low they will tend to be passive and willing to let fate (like a flip of a coin) decide the conflict. When the stakes are moderate, they will permit a third party judgment to decide the conflict, and, finally, when the stakes are high, they will actively engage in a win-lose confrontation or power struggle.*

In the line-staff relationships in Plant Y, it seems that conflict was usually resolved through either a third party resolution by levels higher in the organization or through a win-lose confrontation.

---

[31] Guest, *Organizational Change,* Chapter 9.

[32] Robert R. Blake, Herbert Shepard, and Jane Mouton, *Managing Intergroup Conflict in Industry* (Houston: Gulf Publishing Company, 1964).

THE PLANT Y CASE

Take on this business of not getting the right materials on the line at the right time. A line like this depends upon good material flow. A shortage holds up the operator. The foreman asks the operator, "Why the holdup?" The foreman comes to me about it. I call the material department. First time they ever heard about it. Say they'll check. Nothing happens. I go look for myself. My foreman in the meantime is getting into other trouble, and I'm not around to help.

Inspection

In most sections of the line there were inspection check points manned by inspectors who were ultimately responsible to the chief inspector, not to the section foreman or to other production supervisors. The pattern here paralleled that of material/production relationships. Lateral communications were limited to accusations and defenses, with one party or the other at any given level making a point and not engaging in sustained discussions as to the long-range solution of a given quality problem. The general tendency was for each to have the problem solved by submitting the matter to higher authority through channels. Although "run your own show" was constantly stressed by higher management, most supervisors expressed the need to be in close touch with inspection to gain a fuller understanding of quality requirements. They also complained that line inspectors made judgments that were inconsistent with those in final inspection.

Vroom and Yetton[33] have developed a model of decision-making style that attempts to help managers in a given situation determine the form and amount of participation in decision making by subordinates. They identify four decision methods that can be used by a leader— autocratic, consultative, group, and delegation. These styles correspond to the "telling," "selling," "participating," and "delegating" styles suggested by Situational Leadership Theory.[34]

While Hersey and Blanchard use the task-relevant maturity of one's followers as the main diagnostic dimension for determining appropriate leadership style, Vroom and Yetton use the quality or rationality of the decision, the acceptance by subordinates needed to execute the decision effectively, and the amount of time required to make the decision.

Both these models suggest that an effective manager should use different decision making or leadership styles depending upon the situation. And yet, in Plant Y during this period of disintegration, Stewart and other managers throughout the organization tended to use only autocratic or "telling" (high task/low relationship) styles in all situations. The result was deteriorating human resources (intervening variables[35]) and decreasing "interpersonal competence."[36]

---

[33] Victor H. Vroom and Philip Yetton, *Leadership and Decision Making* (Pittsburgh: University of Pittsburgh Press, 1973).

[34] Hersey and Blanchard, *Management of Organizational Behavior*, 4th ed., Chapter 7.

[35] Likert, *The Human Organization*.

[36] Argyris, "Interpersonal Barriers," and *Interpersonal Competence*.

THE PLANT Y CASE

Work Standards and Comptroller

These same observations applied as well to the other control functions. The work standards department, in the foreman's judgment, "dictated" precisely how a foreman should distribute the work load of his hourly workers without getting the foreman's opinion. The accounting department issued general reports telling the foreman that his efficiency was poor without giving him specific information as to where and why. The production scheduling group changed schedules without due consideration of the current manpower situation.

Telling a foreman that his quality was poor, that his efficiency was low, and that his manpower was "out of line" did nothing, in his judgment, to help him solve his day-to-day operating problems.

Thus, the emerging pattern of staff-line relationships and vertical relationships throughout Plant Y was one of antagonism mixed with fear, discouragement, and distrust.

Under Stewart, Plant Y had become an organization not only with declining performance but also deteriorating human resources when compared with the five other similar assembly plants. Direct labor costs, indirect labor costs, and quality performance are all indicators that the output variables, in Likert's terms, were low, and overall productivity in Plant Y was on a decline. At the same time, safety record, labor grievances, absenteeism, and turnover are all indicators that the "intervening variables" (the condition of the human resources) are in poor condition.[37]

---

[37] Likert, *The Human Organization*. Plant Y would also be considered in poor "organizational health" in Bennis's terms as it lacked *adaptability* or problem-solving ability, it had no clearly defined *identity* that people at all levels could understand and accept, and it had no adequate techniques for *reality testing* to help its management perceive its world correctly. See Warren G. Bennis, *Beyond Bureaucracy: Essays on the Development and Evolution of Human Organizations* (New York: McGraw-Hill Book Company, 1973), pp. 52–54.

V. PLANT Y PERFORMANCE—PERIOD I

Plant Y's comparative record was as follows:

Direct labor costs: Plant Y's efficiency was the poorest among the six plants of the division; it was utilizing 16 percent more direct labor personnel than was called for by divisionwide standards.

Indirect labor costs: Costs of operating the material, maintenance, inspection, and other nonproduction departments were considerably higher than in any other plant in the division.

Quality performance: Based on records of dealer complaints, inspection checks from fabricating divisions, and internal final inspection counts, Plant Y was not only exceeding the maximum standard of defects and rejections set by the division, but it had the poorest quality record among all six plants.

Safety record: Plant Y alternated between last and next-to-last place in the division in the ratio of its monthly lost-time accidents per one hundred employees.

Labor grievances: The average number of formal grievances per one hundred employees was substantially higher than that of the other plants in the division.

Absenteeism: Short-term personal absenteeism was the highest among all the plants.

Turnover: The average monthly rate of quits and discharges was six percent. In numbers it sometimes ran from three hundred to four hundred per month, double the turnover rate recorded for the average of the other five plants.

ANALYSIS

The evidence indicates that the poor performance of Plant Y cannot be attributed to external factors. In that case, Likert would suggest that top management would be more successful in turning the situation around if they attempted first to modify the end-result variables through efforts to change one or more of the causal variables (that is, the plant manager, the management style and expectations of people in the corporate headquarters, and so on) than if they endeavored to alter the intervening variables.[38]

---

[38] Likert, *The Human Organization*, p. 77.

The consistently poor performance of Plant Y, when compared with the performance of other similar plants in the division, can hardly be accounted for by chance. Nor is there any evidence to indicate that the poor record of performance was a function of the plant's geographical location or of economic and market conditions that would affect it alone and not the other plants.

(If reading the case for the first time, skip now to Chapter 3.)

VI. SUMMARY THEORETICAL ANALYSIS
OF THE CONDITIONS IN PLANT Y—PERIOD I

Its performance during this period suggests that Plant Y is spiraling downward and rapidly becoming a very unproductive and ineffective organization. It is obvious that it is not operating as a fully functioning and healthy social system since none of its interrelated parts seems to be either well managed as subsystems or effectively interacting with each other. A summary theoretical analysis of the conditions in Plant Y at this time should give further support to this contention.

In presenting this summary, three categories will be examined: Motivation and behavior, leadership, and change. The analysis presented in this section will include both the theories we have already discussed as well as ones that have not been mentioned. When an analysis is made using a theory that has already been discussed, only brief remarks will be made. When a new theory is introduced, a summary of the theory will be presented before it is used to analyze any aspect of the case.

A. Motivation

Maslow[39]/Hierarchy of Needs

Most members of the management hierarchy were operating at the safety or security need level. Since there were few opportunities in Plant Y during this period for individuals to satisfy social, esteem, or self-actualization needs, little attention seemed to be directed toward these upper level needs.

---

[39] Maslow, *Motivation and Personality.*

SUMMARY ANALYSIS

Herzberg[40]/Motivation-Hygiene Theory

The high rate of dissatisfaction in Plant Y was due to negative hygiene factors, such as lack of job security, poor working conditions, punitive supervision, and deteriorating interpersonal relations. Many of these hygiene factors were still not being taken care of adequately. There was great dissatisfaction in the system, and the **motivators,** *such as recognition for accomplishment and challenging work, seemed to be having little impact.*

McClelland[41]/Achievement-Motivation

McClelland and his associates have been studying for years the need for achievement as a distinct human need. According to their research, people with a high need for achievement have certain characteristics in common. First, they like to set their own goals; they don't respond well to goals unless they are involved in setting them. Second, in establishing their own goals, they tend to set moderately difficult but potentially achievable goals, that is, goals that are achievable but hard enough to "stretch" them. Third, they seem to be more concerned with personal achievement than with the rewards of success. As a result, they are more interested in concrete feedback on how well they are performing (task-relevant feedback) than they are in attitudinal feedback about their personal characteristics, such as how cooperative or helpful they are.

[40] Frederick Herzberg, Bernard Mausner, and Barbara Snyderman, *The Motivation to Work* (New York: John Wiley and Sons, Inc., 1959), and Herzberg, *Work and the Nature of Man* (New York: World Publishing Co., 1966).

[41] David C. McClelland, J. W. Atkinson, R. A. Clark, and E. L. Lowell, *The Achievement Motive* (New York: Appleton-Century-Crofts, 1953), and *The Achieving Society* (Princeton, N.J.: D. Van Nostrand Co., Inc., 1961).

Period of Disintegration

Given these characteristics, one might suggest that Plant Y would not have been a satisfying place to work for an achievement-motivated person. Unrealistic goals were being set in an environment that did not permit most managers to play a role in goal setting nor receive concrete task-relevant feedback. The fact is that several supervisors simply quit.

Homans/Activities-Interactions-Sentiments

Homans[42] of the interactionist school developed a model of human groups. According to this model, certain activities, interactions, and sentiments are essential (or required) for the group to get its work done. In other words, jobs (activities) have to be performed that require people to work together (interactions). As people interact they begin to develop certain attitudes (sentiments) toward one another. If the sentiments that develop among people during their **required** activities and interactions are positive, new or **emergent** activities will evolve among the group members. They eat lunch together, form bowling teams, and so on. They interact more and build further on their already positive sentiments. The group tends to develop expectations or **norms** that specify how people in the group "should" behave under specific circumstances. If, however, negative sentiments emerge in the course of getting the job done (required activities and interaction), then no mutually supportive norms develop.

In Plant Y, managers and staff personnel seem to be engaging only in a base minimum of activities and interactions required to get the job done. The system has created negative sentiments within the management hierarchy. The only norm that seems to have developed is "cover up and protect yourself." Top-down pressure and the use of punitive control mechanisms preclude the development of norms that would sanction creativity, enthusiasm, and mutual support in solving problems.

---

[42] Homans, The Human Group.

Guest, also taking the interactionists' approach, observed the inter-action patterns in Plant Y and found that the "period of disintegration" was characterized by a:

> communications system in which a high proportion of interactions were originated by superiors to subordinates. Expressed sentiments about one's relationship to others and about conditions in general were extremely negative. Performance [activities] was inferior . . . when contrasted with the performance of other similar plants.[43]

Argyris[44]/Immaturity-Maturity Theory

According to Argyris, as individuals develop from children into mature people over the years, they move from (1) a passive state to one of increasing activity; (2) a state of dependency upon others to a state of relative independence; (3) behaving in only a few ways to being capable of behaving in many ways; (4) erratic, casual, and shallow interests to deeper commitments and interests; (5) a short, present time perspective to a longer time perspective, which includes the past as well as the future; (6) a position subordinate to everyone to an equal or superior position with others; and (7) a lack of awareness of a "self" to an awareness of and ability to control "self." Argyris postulates that these changes reside on a continuum and that the "healthy" personality develops along the continuum from "immaturity" to "maturity."

People at Plant Y, of course, were not children, but curiously enough they manifested behavior that Argyris would put at the immature end of the continuum. They exerted minimal control over their environment. They became passive, dependent, and subordinate. They saw few alternatives open to them other than conforming.

---

[43] Guest, *Organizational Change*, p. 104.
[44] Argyris, *Integrating the Individual and the Organization* (New York: John Wiley and Sons, Inc., 1965).

Berne[45] and Harris[46]/Transactional Analysis

Transactional Analysis (TA) is another method of analyzing and understanding human behavior. There are three concepts from TA that are useful in examining the conditions at Plant Y at the end of Period I: (1) ego states, (2) life positions, and (3) "stroking."

According to TA, all people have, in differing degrees, three ego states—child, parent, and adult. As Berne states, "Although we cannot directly observe these ego states, we can observe behavior and from this infer which of the three ego states is operating at that moment."[47]

The child ego state is associated with behaviors that are evoked when a person reacts from a purely emotional base. This state is manifest in "natural" impulses and attitudes learned from child experiences. There are three types of child ego states. The **natural child** *is uninhibited, joyful, spontaneous, and free. The* **adapted child** *conforms to parent wishes and desires. He or she does what is expected. The* **little professor** *contains the beginning of the adult ego state; it learns to mediate between the wishes of the natural child and the adapted child.*

The parent ego state is a result of the kind of conditioning (set of "recordings") people received from their parents, siblings, teachers, and other powerful figures in their early childhood. A person operates from a parent ego state when he or she plays back "old tapes" that say such things as "It's right! It's wrong!," "It's bad! It's good!" or "I should! I shouldn't!" It's the **evaluative** *part of us. The two main kinds of parent ego states are* **nurturing parent** *and* **critical parent.**

The adult ego state evokes rational, problem-solving behavior. People operating from the adult ego state are taking the emotional content

---

[45] Eric Berne, *Games People Play* (New York: Grove Press, Inc., 1964).

[46] Thomas Harris, *I'm OK—You're OK: A Practical Guide to Transactional Analysis* (New York: Harper and Row, Publishers, 1969).

[47] Eric Berne, *Principles of Group Treatment* (New York: Oxford University Press, 1964), p. 281.

60

of their child ego state and the value-laden content of their parent ego state and checking them out in the external world. They are examining alternatives and probable outcomes and engaging in problem-solving analysis and rational decision making.

According to TA, all of us tend to operate in these three ego states at different times. A healthy individual maintains a good balance among all three. And yet, many people seem dominated at times by one or two of them. These TA concepts may have some relevance to what happened to the management of Plant Y during the "period of disintegration."

Much of the managerial behavior in Plant Y seems to reflect the adapted child ("I just go ahead and do it!") or the critical parent ("You better do that" or "You shouldn't do that!"). On the other hand, there appears to be little evidence of behavior being evoked from **adult** ego states (problem solving and rational decision making). The absence of any real "adult" behavior signals a rapidly deteriorating human organization. It is caught in win-lose confrontations and competition and is unable to engage in cooperative and rational problem solving.

TA also suggests that people have some basic attitude sets that help mold their personalities. These "life positions" are depicted all the way from "I'm OK, you're OK" to "I'm not OK, you're not OK," with interim positions of "I'm OK, you're not OK" and "I'm not OK, you're OK." In Plant Y we see a definite shift from the "OK" positions to the "not OK" positions as the environment becomes dominated by punishment and fear rather than supportive behavior. The most widespread life positions under Stewart seem to be either "I'm OK, you're not OK" or "I'm not OK, you're not OK."

Another postulate of TA is "stroking." Everyone needs to be "in contact" with other people to be recognized as an individual. Most people want and need "positive" strokes that reassure them about their personal worth or provide feedback about their competencies.

In Plant Y under Stewart the environment is becoming overwhelmed by "negative" strokes. There were almost no "positive" strokes *available at any level of the management hierarchy. The situation became so critical that people were trying to avoid any interaction with their boss at all. It was a "punishment-centered" environment.*

B. Leadership (Attitudinal and Behavioral)

Blake, Shepard and Mouton[48]/Model for Managing Intergroup Conflict

At every level of the management hierarchy, the predominant attitudinal set about conflict seemed to be "conflict is inevitable/agreement is impossible." Thus, most attempts at conflict resolution were through third party interventions and win-lose power struggles.

McGregor[49]/Theory X-Theory Y

As suggested by the analysis of Plant Y using Argyris's Immaturity-Maturity Theory, the basic assumptions about human nature that prevailed under Stewart were Theory X. Some of the lower level managers suggested that they had positive assumptions (Theory Y) about people, but everyone seemed to treat their subordinates as if they were lazy, unreliable, and irresponsible.

Argyris[50]/XA-YB

There seems to be little doubt that the prevailing behavior pattern among managers throughout the hierarchy was A—controlling, direct, close

---

48 Blake, Shepard, and Mouton, *Managing Intergroup Conflict.*
49 McGregor, *The Human Side of Enterprise.*
50 Argyris, *Management and Organizational Development.*

supervision. *Stewart's comments and behavior suggest that he was an XA manager. As implied in the McGregor discussion, some of the lower level managers under the top-down pressure may have been YA managers. During this period of disintegration, there certainly did not appear to be any managers with B behavior patterns—supportive, "participative" general supervision—regardless of whether they had X or Y assumptions about people.*

Tannenbaum-Schmidt[51]/Leadership Continuum

In discussing leader behavior, Tannenbaum and Schmidt depicted a broad range of styles on a continuum moving from authoritarian leader behavior at one end to democratic leader behavior at the other. Leaders whose behavior is observed to be at the authoritarian end of the continuum tend to tell their followers what to do and how to do it, while leaders whose behavior appears to be at the democratic end tend to share their leadership responsibilities with their followers by involving them in the planning and execution of the task.

The leadership style throughout the management hierarchy of Plant Y was predominantly authoritarian with little sharing of leadership responsibilities with followers.

Michigan Leadership Studies[52]

In the early studies of the Survey Research Center at the University of Michigan, two leadership concepts, which they called **employee orien-**

---

[51] Robert Tannenbaum and Warren H. Schmidt, "How to Choose a Leadership Pattern," *Harvard Business Review* (March–April 1957), pp. 95–101.

[52] D. Katz, N. Maccoby, and Nancy C. Morse, *Productivity, Supervision, and Morale in an Office Situation* (Ann Arbor, Mich.: Survey Research Center, 1950), and D. Katz, N. Maccoby, G. Gurin, and Lucretia G. Floor, *Productivity, Supervision, and Morale Among Railroad Workers* (Ann Arbor, Mich.: Survey Research Center, 1951).

tation *and* production orientation, *seemed to be related to each other and tests of effectiveness. They found that employee-oriented leaders feel that every employee is important. Therefore, they take interest in everyone, accepting their individuality and personal needs. On the other hand, production-oriented leaders emphasized production, viewing employees as tools to accomplish the goals of the organization.*

At Plant Y under Stewart, there seemed to be a high emphasis on production-orientation with little concern for employee-orientation.

Cartwright and Zander[53]/Group Dynamics Studies

Based on the findings of numerous studies, Cartwright and Zander claim that all group objectives fall into one of two categories: (1) the achievement of some specific group goal, or (2) the maintenance or strengthening of the group itself.

The tremendous top-down pressure and low morale in Plant Y suggest that goal achievement *was the main concern of Stewart, while he paid little attention to* group maintenance.

Ohio State Leadership Studies[54]

The staff of the Bureau of Business Research at Ohio State University, composed of such well-known behavioral scientists as Coons, Fleishmann, Halpin, Hemphill, and Stogdill, narrowed the description of leader behavior to two dimensions: Initiating Structure *and* Consideration. *Initiating structure refers to "the leader's behavior in delineating the relationship between himself and members of the work group and in*

[53] Dorwin Cartwright and Alvin Zander, eds., *Group Dynamics: Research and Theory*, 2nd ed. (Evanston, Ill.: Row, Peterson and Co., 1960).

[54] Roger M. Stogdill and Alvin E. Coons, eds., *Leader Behavior: Its Description and Measurement*, Research Monograph No. 88 (Columbus: Bureau of Business Research, The Ohio State University, 1957).

THE PLANT Y CASE

endeavoring to establish well-defined patterns of organization, channels of communication, and methods of procedure." On the other hand, consideration refers to "behavior indicative of friendship, mutual trust, respect, and warmth in the relationship between the leader and the members of his staff."[55] Situational Leadership Theory (Hersey and Blanchard[56]) is an outgrowth of the leadership model developed at Ohio State University.

In terms of Initiating Structure and Consideration, the predominant leadership style used in Plant Y was high structure/low consideration. Although this style was the intent of Stewart and others, the high structure was seen more as punitive than as establishing well-defined patterns of organization, channels of communication, and methods of procedure.

Blake and Mouton[57]/The Managerial Grid

In the Managerial Grid, Blake and Mouton identify five different types of leadership based on concern for production and concern for people. The five leadership styles are labeled as follows:

1. **Task** *(high concern for production/low concern for people).*
2. **Team** *(high concern for both production and people).*
3. **Country Club** *(high concern for people/low concern for production).*
4. **Impoverished** *(low concern for both production and people).*
5. **Middle-of-the-Road** *(moderate concern for both production and people).*

---

[55] Andrew W. Halpin, *The Leadership Behavior of School Superintendents* (Chicago: Midwest Administration Center, The University of Chicago, 1959), p. 4.

[56] Hersey and Blanchard, *Management of Organizational Behavior*, Chapter 7.

[57] Robert R. Blake and Jane S. Mouton, *The Managerial Grid* (Houston: Gulf Publishing Company, 1964).

The management of Plant Y, particularly Stewart and the top management in division headquarters, seemed to have a "task" management attitude; that is they demonstrated a high concern for production but a low concern for people. The lower level managers claimed they did not have this same attitude and then behaved as if they did. While this task management prevailed, some managers seemed to have moved to an "impoverished" attitude. Being concerned only with "protecting themselves," they showed little concern for production or people.

Likert[58]/Patterns of Management

Using the earlier Michigan studies as a starting place, Rensis Likert did some extensive research to discover the general pattern of management used by high producing managers in contrast to other managers. He found that the tendency is for supervisors with the best records of performance to be "employee-centered"—they endeavored to build effective work groups with high performance goals. Other supervisors who kept constant pressure on production were called "job-centered" and were found more often to have low producing sections. Likert also found that general rather than close supervision tended to be associated with high productivity. The management of Plant Y under Stewart was clearly "job-centered" and tended to use close supervision.

In later studies, Likert[59] found that the prevailing management styles used in organizations can be depicted on a continuum from System 1 through System 4. In essence, System 1 is a task-oriented, highly structured authoritarian management style; System 4 is a relationship-oriented management style based on teamwork, mutual trust, and confidence. Systems 2 and 3 are intermediate stages between two extremes, which approximate closely Theory X and Theory Y assumptions.

---

[58] Rensis Likert, *New Patterns of Management* (New York: McGraw-Hill Book Company, 1961), pp. 7–9.

[59] Likert, *The Human Organization.*

In terms of Likert's continuum of management styles, Plant Y was at the System 1 end of the continuum. This is particularly evident when one looks at events in Plant Y under Stewart in light of some of the System 1 items on Likert's Profile of Organizational Characteristics instrument,[60] which he uses to identify the prevailing management style being used in an organization (see Table 1).

Table 1 A comparison between events occurring in Plant Y "before change" and System 1 items modified from Likert's *Profile of Organizational Characteristics*.

Likert's System One	Plant Y Before Change
Management is seen as having no confidence or trust in subordinates.	Meetings called to handle emergencies; manager gives orders, asks questions; subordinates do not talk to each other, discuss, or make suggestions.
Control lies in top management; subordinates seldom involved in decision making; bulk of decisions and goal setting made at top and issued down chain of command.	Division tells plant manager what to do in each crisis; plant manager tells supervisors what to do.
Subordinates forced to work with fear, punishment, and only occasional rewards.	Plant manager "chews out" foremen; general foremen punish section foremen. "If you can't do it, get out."
Superiors see subordinates as being motivated primarily by physiological and safety needs.	
The little superior-subordinate interaction that does take place seems to be characterized by fear and mistrust.	Plant manager plays back tapes of his meetings to division manager to prove his obedience to orders; "I just say yes, sir."

[60] Ibid., pp. 4–10.

Fiedler[61]/Leadership Contingency Model

According to a Leadership Contingency Model developed by Fiedler, there is no "best" leadership style. It is not a matter of the best style but of the most effective style for a particular situation. Fiedler has found in his research that there are three major variables that seem to determine whether a given situation is favorable or unfavorable to leaders: (1) their personal relations with the members of their group (leader-member relations); (2) the degree of structure in the task that the group has been assigned to perform (task structure); and (3) the power and authority that their position provides (position power). In his research, these three dimensions of the leaders' situation were combined into a single scale. Situations ranged from most favorable (where the leader is well liked by group members, has a powerful position, and is directing a well-defined job) to least favorable (where the leader is disliked, has little position power, and faces an unstructured task) for the leader.

Fiedler has attempted through his research to determine what the most effective leadership style—task-oriented or relationships-oriented—seems to be in various situations. He has found that task-oriented leaders are successful in situations that are either favorable or unfavorable to the leader, while relationship-oriented leaders are successful in situations in between, neither favorable nor unfavorable for the leader.

The "favorableness" of the situation in Plant Y was **intermediate** *for Stewart since he had moderate-to-high-position power (he could hire and fire, influence salary increments, and such) and task structure (he was generally supervising managers of jobs that were well defined and spelled out) but poor leader-member relations (he was disliked and not trusted). For such a situation, the theory would have recommended a relationship-oriented leadership style. Yet Stewart used the opposite style— task-oriented. Although this style might have been appropriate earlier, when Stewart first assumed his present position at Plant Y, it now seems*

---

[61] Fred E. Fiedler, *A Theory of Leadership Effectiveness* (New York: McGraw-Hill Company, 1967).

to be having diminishing returns. Since then, even his position power is being eroded by lack of confidence from headquarters, and now the probability of any style used by Stewart being effective is questionable. A similar analysis could be made for other managers throughout the hierarchy in Plant Y.

Lawrence and Lorsch[62]/Differentiation and Integration Model

According to Lawrence and Lorsch, there is no "best" way to design an organization. The design of the organization and its subsystems must "fit" its environment. The needs of individual organizational members as well as the organization itself are better satisfied to the extent that the organization is properly designed. In examining organizational design, they look at two concepts: differentiation and integration. "Differentiation" is the **differences in cognitive and emotional orientations among managers in different functional departments, and the differences in formal structure among these departments.** *Thus, each department, whether it be sales, research, or production, is a subsystem in which members would develop particular orientation and structural tasks, depending on their task and their predispositions.*

"Integration" is the **quality of the state of collaboration that exists among departments that are required to achieve unity of effort by the environment.** *In a complex organization such as Plant Y, there was a need for a high level of both* **differentiation** *between subunits as well as* **integration** *among them. Yet, integration was low because of a poor communication system throughout the management hierarchy (the* **basic** *organizational mechanism for achieving integration). Communication channels seemed to be only one way, from the top down, with little two-way or multiway communication back up the hierarchy or horizontally between departments and subunits. There seemed to be more competition than collaboration, more "holding back" than sharing.*

---

[62] P. R. Lawrence and J. W. Lorsch, *Organization and Environment: Managing Differentiation and Integration* (Boston: Dir. of Research, Harvard Business School, 1967).

Period of Disintegration　　　　　　　　　　　　　　　　**69**

Hersey and Blanchard[63]/Situational Leadership Theory

The predominant leadership being used by management in Plant Y was high task/low relationship ("telling") with little evidence of flexibility. The continual use of this style was resented by people and seemed inappropriate since the lower level managers had been willing and able previously to take responsibility for goal accomplishment (moderate maturity) based on their past experience and record. If this inappropriate style is continually used, it leads to a self-fulfilling prophecy—that is, if one repeatedly treats people as if they were less mature than they are, eventually an effective cycle will begin to develop in which low expectations result in low performance, which reinforces the low expectations and causes even lower productivity.

Change

Lewin[64]/Force Field Analysis

Lewin argues that in any situation there are both driving and restraining forces that influence any change that may occur. **Driving forces** *are those forces affecting a situation that are pushing in a particular direction; they tend to initiate a change and keep it going. In terms of improving performance in Plant Y, pressure from division headquarters, close, punitive supervision by Stewart, and job insecurity are examples of driving forces.* **Restraining forces** *are forces acting to restrain or decrease the driving forces. Resentment, fear, lack of coordination, "buck passing," deterioration of the plant and equipment, and "short-circuiting" the*

---

[63] Hersey and Blanchard, *Management of Organizational Behavior*, 4th ed., Chapter 7.

[64] Kurt Lewin, "Frontiers in Group Dynamics: Concept, Method and Reality in Social Science, Social Equilibria and Social Change," *Human Relations*, I, No. 1 (June 1947), 5–41. See also *Field Theory in Social Science*, ed. D. Cartwright (New York: Harper and Brothers, 1951).

THE PLANT Y CASE

chain of command are all examples of restraining forces that are working against increased production in Plant Y.

Lewin found that equilibrium is reached in an organization when the sum of the driving forces equals the sum of the restraining forces. This equilibrium, or present level of productivity, can be raised or lowered by changes in the relationship between the driving and restraining forces. In Plant Y the present level of productivity was continuing to decline because the driving forces pushing for increased productivity are being overpowered by the restraining forces. No matter how much top-down pressure is exerted by division headquarters or Stewart, it had little impact on all the restraining forces that had built up in the internal system.

Hersey and Blanchard[65]/Change Cycles

Hersey and Blanchard discuss two different change cycles—the participative change cycle and the coerced change cycle. As is evident in the case, Stewart is attempting to increase the productivity of Plant Y by using coercive change methods, which emphasize the use of position power and close supervision. This method seems to be "backfiring" because of the build-up of animosity and hostility.

Kelman[66]/Mechanisms for Change

Managers are being forced through compliance to identify with coercive, high task/low relationship ("telling") managerial models. The result is a gradual **internalization** of these styles as the need levels of managers move to job security and survival.

---

[65] Hersey and Blanchard, *Management of Organizational Behavior*, Chapter 10.
[66] Kelman, "Compliance, Identification."

Guest[67]/Sociotechnical Cycle Theory

Interruptions in work flow, mechanical breakdowns, scheduling mix-ups, crowded equipment layouts, problems of tooling and material flow all combined to set in motion a series of human confrontations marked by interpersonal conflict and tension. Such human reaction to technological malfunctions had a "self-feeding" cyclical effect. The rational solution of purely technical problems decreased as the "irrational" human confrontations increased.

---

[67] Guest, *Organizational Change*, Chapter 9.

With the declining intervening variables and poor performance, top management decided to make a change in one of the important causal variables (Likert[1])—the plant manager. In some ways they had little choice. The spiraling down performance and morale in Plant Y had reached the point where it could not be turned around in a short period because of the large reservoir of negative past experience that had built up in the organization. Much of the focus and energy was directed toward perceived problems in the environment, such as interpersonal relations and respect for supervision rather than toward the work itself. Reaction to what Herzberg[2] would call "deteriorating hygiene factors" took such form as hostility, "name calling," and a general breakdown in work performance. When this happens, even if a manager like Stewart actually changed his behavior and "took the heat off," the credibility gap based on long-term experience is such that the response will still be distrust and skepticism rather than change.

---

[1] Rensis Likert, *The Human Organization* (New York: McGraw-Hill Book Company, 1967).

[2] Frederick Herzberg, *Work and the Nature of Man* (New York: World Publishing Co., 1966).

THE PLANT Y CASE

I. SUCCESSION OF A NEW MANAGER

An unofficial and costly walkout prompted divisional and corporate executives to do something about the deteriorating situation at Plant Y. Some executives thought that middle and lower management personnel were not competent. Others thought that radical labor leaders might be causing the problem. Still others took the position that a man with "strong leadership traits" was needed and that he should "clean house." It was flatly stated that unless things changed, "We're going to shut the plant down." In the end, they decided to assign Matthew Cooley* to manage the plant. Cooley was the production manager at another plant and had worked under a plant manager who had, it was said, "a good track record." Reflecting on Cooley's appointment, the executive vice-president of the corporation later observed:

> We have a lot of managerial talent and backup in our corporation. We insist on managerial development. Cooley was only one among many candidates. He looked good but not head and shoulders above others we could have selected.

Cooley was called on Thursday and told to report to Plant Y as manager the following Monday. Stewart, the current plant manager, resigned under any early pension retirement arrangement.

---

*Cooley recalled that in his university days he had studied under the famous American sociologist, Charles H. Cooley, who was the leading pioneer in the study of primary groups and their importance in understanding human behavior. This explains the pseudonym "Matt Cooley" given to the plant manager by Guest in his writing of the case.

Thus, *if change was to occur, it seemed necessary to bring in a new manager from the outside. The reason this had a higher probability of success is that the sum of the past experiences of the managers in Plant Y with the new manager, Cooley, would be likened to a "clean slate," and thus any different behaviors he demonstrated in efforts to change things at the plant would be on a much more believable basis.*[3]

In examining change, Lewin[4] identified three phases of the change process: unfreezing, changing, and refreezing.

The aim of **unfreezing** *is to motivate and make the individual or the group ready to change. It is a "thawing out" process where the forces acting on an individual are rearranged so that now he or she sees the need for change.*

Cooley began the unfreezing process at the introductory dinner by two means: (1) arranging the seating so that the old cliques were broken up to remove people from their accustomed sources of information and social relationships, and (2) circulating among the lower level managers after dinner rather than staying with top management, which for some lower level managers symbolized that he was interested in obtaining some personal power with them and not always relying on position power as Stewart had.

Guest[5] stresses the importance of symbolic acts at the beginning of the change process. Such acts have no immediate effects on the behavior or performance of the members of the organization, but they set the stage for later substantive action by the manager.

---

[3] This discussion is expanded in Paul Hersey and Kenneth H. Blanchard, *Management of Organizational Behavior: Utilizing Human Resources,* 4th ed. (Englewood Cliffs, N.J.: Prentice-Hall, Inc., 1977), Chapter 6.

[4] Kurt Lewin, "Frontiers in Group Dynamics: Concept, Method, and Reality in Social Science; Social Equilibria and Social Change," *Human Relations,* I, No. 1 (June 1947), 5–41.

[5] Robert H. Guest, *Organizational Change: The Effect of Successful Leadership* (Homewood, Ill.: The Dorsey Press, Inc. and Richard D. Irwin, Inc., 1962), pp. 110–11.

When asked later what instructions he received from headquarters, Cooley said:

> The division manager assured me that I could ask for any
> new personnel that I needed, that he would back me up and
> that I was to "clear out the dead wood." That's all. I didn't
> have any master plan prepared.

When Cooley arrived at Plant Y accompanied by the division manager, an introductory dinner meeting was held in a
hotel near the plant. The meeting was attended by all members
of the managerial organization down through the foremen, more
than 300 in all. As one of the general foremen described it a
week after the meeting:

> When I went to this dinner meeting the first thing that
> struck me was the way they had the seating arrangement. I
> think it was done very well. Whoever arranged it made sure that
> the old cliques they had in supervision were broken up. We also
> noticed that the new plant manager sat down among the
> foremen and general foremen. The vice-president (actually, the
> division manager) of the division introduced us to the new
> manager. The vice-president said something about his confidence
> in the new manager. We can remember when an earlier
> manager came here, and he got rid of a whole lot of people in
> supervision. He just gave them their walking papers and sent
> them on their way. We wondered what the new man was going
> to do.
>
> We expected that the new plant manager would probably
> hang around the division manager after the meeting was over.
> Big shots usually stick together, but he didn't. He just kept
> circulating on the floor and meeting as many of the guys as he
> could. I was quite surprised, and so were the others.

Guest[6] *in his earlier analysis of Plant Y utilized some concepts of McGregor*[7] *to illustrate how Cooley, right from the beginning, was attempting to use his authority in a way to integrate the needs of the organization and the needs of the people. McGregor emphasizes that the power of a manager does not just come from position or from consent by subordinates (people power) but by a* **collaborative process of goal attainment.** *Success may be achieved when the job requirements of leaders and followers are "set by the* **situation;** *they need not be seen by either party as personal requirements established by the superior."*[8]

Under Stewart, because of the high concern for security, supervisors had felt they could not act on the basis of rational decision making but **had** *to act on the basis of their perception of what they thought the manager personally wanted. He acted similarly toward his divisional superiors. Cooley began immediately by setting some basic goals, but then moved quickly to focusing on concerns that the supervisors were having. He acted as if his power stemmed from the kinds of contributions he was in a position to make in helping them solve their problems and do a better job. He seemed to want to create an environment where supervisors could respond to a "situation" (not just to their "boss") and to what McGregor called their "interdependence," that is, he needed them as much as they needed him to get this plant "back on its feet."*

---

[6] Ibid., pp. 122–23.

[7] Douglas McGregor as cited in Warren G. Bennis, "Leadership Theory and Administrative Behavior," *Administrative Science Quarterly*, 4, No. 3 (December 1959), 259–301.

[8] Ibid., p. 260.

THE PLANT Y CASE

CASE

    His first few days at the plant were spent getting acquainted with his staff and "sounding them out" on problem areas. In the first meeting with all supervision, he put forward what he called "a few basic goals" for the organization in terms of expected efficiency and quality. He stated candidly to the group that Plant Y had a bad reputation. He said he had heard that many members of supervision were not capable of doing their jobs. He said, "I am willing to prove that this is not so, and until shown otherwise I personally have full confidence in the group." He went on to say that his job was "not to catch and punish people for doing a poor job, but rather to help them in any way he could to do a good job." He also stated, "I don't believe in firing a lot of people and using threats and fear."

ANALYSIS

By opening up suggestions by foremen and the union committee, Cooley was begining to adopt a "consultative" style (Vroom and Yetton[9]). He was symbolizing a change from Stewart's punitive style. Yet Cooley was not changing too drastically to "high relationship/low task" (Hersey and Blanchard[10]). That is, he was keeping a high degree of "structure" in the situation by setting goals and giving directions. He was simultaneously tackling the problem of pervasive insecurity (Maslow[11]). He was also reinforcing his belief that his people were "OK" (Berne[12]), that he did not intend to vest all power at the top, that he was making Theory Y assumptions (McGregor[13]), and that he wanted to be perceived as exercising "personal power" as distinguished from raw "position power."[14] Such supportive relationships were legitimate (Likert[15]).

It is also interesting to note that Cooley was going to maintain and support the organizational structure; he did not want to negotiate with the union, but he was going to open up the channels of communication. He told the union in essence, that "we have a legal, negotiated contract; we've got to respect that. But over and above that contract, you guys may have some ideas on how to make this plant more productive." He appeared to want his managers and the union to "buy into" ("selling") the idea of getting this organization back on its feet. He definitely had moved from the high task/low relationship style of Stewart almost immediately to high task/high relationship (Hersey and Blanchard[16]).

---

[9] Victor H. Vroom and Philip Yetton, *Leadership and Decision Making* (Pittsburgh: University of Pittsburgh Press, 1973).

[10] Hersey and Blanchard, *Management of Organizational Behavior*, 4th ed., Chapter 7.

[11] Abraham H. Maslow, *Motivation and Personality* (New York: Harper and Row, Publishers, 1954).

[12] Eric Berne, *Games People Play* (New York: Grove Press, Inc., 1964).

[13] Douglas McGregor, *The Human Side of Enterprise* (New York: McGraw-Hill Book Company, 1960).

[14] Amitai Etzioni, *A Comparative Analysis of Complex Organizations* (New York: The Free Press, 1961).

[15] Rensis Likert, *New Patterns of Management* (New York: McGraw-Hill Book Company, 1961).

[16] Hersey and Blanchard, *Management of Organizational Behavior*, 4th ed., Chapter 4.

One of the first steps taken by the new manager was to send a letter to each of the one hundred foremen asking to be invited to their sections. The foremen indicated some surprise, and one of them said: "I guess this new fellow is a pretty good manager. He wants to be invited to come down to inspect my section. I'll be very happy if he does come around."

Also within the first few days, Cooley met with the union shop committee and, after stating a few general objectives, urged them to make any comments they wanted to.

The union president reported the meeting this way:

Cooley was introduced to all of us at a shop committee meeting. He told the committee in straight language just what he believed in and what he hoped to do at Plant Y. He said that before he came in he had been briefed on this plant, and that he had heard it was a lousy plant with lousy people in it, and that he was going to have to cope with this. Then he said that he didn't believe the story one single bit—that in the couple of days he had been around he had found out that the people at Plant Y were okay. He said he was going to operate that way. Then he said that it was not his intention to negotiate on grievances, but that he was inviting us personally to see him any time about ways to make the plant better. He said he welcomed any suggestions.

This was a completely new approach to the committee, and although some of the boys were skeptical, most of us felt that this man meant what he said. What a change!

Here Cooley begins to recognize that there is a need for a systematic planning process at Plant Y, especially if he is to be successful in replacing the crisis management that characterized Stewart's approach.

At first, Cooley starts off with traditional planning theory[17] and ends up with participatory planning theory.[18] In fact, he begins to suggest the implementation of some procedures characteristic of Management By Objectives (MBO).[19] For example, without being explicit, Cooley suggests an informal way of contracting goals and objectives.

Dalton, whose wide-ranging research on how change is initiated and implemented, would be familiar with the implications of Cooley's actions here. Dalton says that a first pattern of action characterizing successful attempts to bring about behavioral and attitudinal change is the way in which leaders move from generalized goals to specific and concrete objectives. Subordinates will not respond over time when goals continue to be perceived as vague and general. Each member of the organization must see how the specifics of change in his or her own area of responsibility are related to the broad goals put forward by a manager.[20]

Here again Cooley, early in the change process, focused on a problem or concern of the supervisors and workers. He did not just talk about the problem or concern; he did something about it. In this case, he was dealing at the most basic level of needs in the Maslow hierarchy—physiological needs.

---

[17] J. D. Mooney and A. C. Reiley, *The Principles of Organization* (New York: Harper and Brothers, 1939). See also Harold Koontz and Cyril O'Donnell, *Principles of Management,* 4th ed. (New York: McGraw-Hill Book Company, 1968).

[18] As an example of some participatory planning, see Peter F. Drucker, *The Practice of Management* (New York: Harper and Row, Publishers, 1954).

[19] For one of the most popular presentations of MBO, see George S. Odiorne, *Management by Objectives* (New York: Pitman Publishing Corp., 1965).

[20] Gene W. Dalton, "Influence and Organizational Change," reprinted in David A. Kolb, Irwin M. Rubin, and James M. McIntyre, *Organizational Psychology: A Book of Readings* (New York: Prentice-Hall, Inc., 1970), pp. 401–25.

During the introductory period, it became evident to Cooley in talks with various people—his immediate staff, operating supervisors, union committeemen, and hourly workers—and in his observations of the physical plant itself, that the organization was, as he put it, "operating from day-to-day on a kind of 'emergency' basis." Except for a certain amount of overall planning at the corporation and division levels, there appeared to be little long-range planning at the local level. He said he recognized that the "cooperate-or-else" philosophy under which the plant had operated previously was not working. He added:

> I saw that the organization needed a long-range program spelled out in writing and reviewed with the department heads, the staff, and superintendents. They needed to be in agreement on something that was realizable and tangible and practical. It had to come from the whole organization and be explained to the whole organization, and for that portion of it which affects the hourly people, the union should be taken into confidence and be told what the long-range objectives would be from the point of view of their membership. Then we had to start moving on it.

One of the first steps taken by Cooley was to get permission from the division to begin reduction of the long overtime hours. As a union officer put it:

> We have had managers come in and give us a lot of soft talk, but they never backed it up. This fellow showed up, and one of the first things he did was to cut down on the long hours which had been going on for months. It had been ragged on the men. I don't know how much the men realized who was responsible, but the committeemen knew it, and they must have passed it on. The average worker, I think, gets a lot of his impressions of management from the committeemen.

ANALYSIS

While no immediate changes in performance occurred, Cooley was reinforcing a more humanistic/democratic value system (the organizational counterpart to Theory Y assumptions about people). By reinforcing these values, not threats and fear, Cooley was creating, as Argyris argues, a "psychologically" safe environment, which generated an increase in interpersonal competence, trust, intergroup cooperation, and organizational problem-solving capabilities.[21]

Stewart had almost never initiated or tried to influence "up" (that is, division headquarters). He just reacted to interactions directed from the top. Cooley, right from the beginning, started to increase the frequency of interactions initiated from Plant Y up to division and corporate headquarters ("interactionists"[22]*).*

Early in the change process, Cooley concentrated on improving the hygiene factors (Herzberg[23]*) and satisfying the physiological and safety needs (Maslow*[24]*) of the members of the organization at all levels. In other words, he began to reduce the areas of dissatisfaction. Theoretically, this strategy seems to make sense because unless the lower level needs and the environmental factors that satisfy these needs are taken care of, people will not be motivated to take on more responsibility in their jobs.*

---

[21] Chris Argyris, "Interpersonal Barriers to Decision-Making," *Harvard Business Review* (22), 2:84–97, 1966, and *Interpersonal Competence and Organizational Effectiveness* (Homewood, Ill.: The Dorsey Press, Inc. and Richard D. Irwin, Inc., 1962).

[22] The main "interactionist" reference used in this text is George C. Homans, *The Human Group* (New York: Harcourt, Brace and Company, 1950).

[23] Herzberg, *Work and the Nature of Man.*

[24] Maslow, *Motivation and Personality.*

In these first two weeks and for many months after, no measurable changes in performance were observed. Nonetheless, Cooley's behavior evoked favorable comment. He had not cleaned house and had said in effect that the plant could solve its own problems without outside help. He set forth a few general goals, but spent most of his time observing technical operations and listening to what others had to say.

II. CHANGES IN THE TECHNICAL SYSTEM

Although Plant Y was one of the oldest of the assembly plants in the division, few physical changes had been requested or made for several years. It was corporation policy to grant funds to all its plants and divisions where there was a proven need and where there was reasonable assurance that the improvements would "pay off." Proof of need and assurance of economic justification rested primarily with the plant manager.

Making changes in these areas, which are tangible (Guest calls them "symbolic"), does several things. It begins to create an environment in which members of the organization begin to believe change is possible and that this leader is capable of making changes. In essence, Cooley was demonstrating to all that, unlike Stewart, he was going to be an effective "linking pin" between Plant Y and divisional headquarters. As Likert argues, "The capacity to exert influence upward is essential if a supervisor (or manager) is to perform his supervisory function successfully. To be effective in leading his own work group, a superior must be able to influence his own boss, that is, he needs to be skilled both as a supervisor and as a subordinate."[25] Making tangible environmental changes "buys time" for the change agent; this is especially important in this case since Cooley seems to have decided to emphasize participative change methods,[26] which require personal power and take much longer than coercive techniques. As Likert[27] has found, rebuilding an organization from System 1 to System 4 takes time depending upon the size and complexity of the organization.

This again illustrates that it takes time to create new norms of behavior. The personnel in Plant Y had a long history of maintenance deterioration, which resulted in no one caring. Cooley's actions here symbolized that things were going to be different. He was not going to let things "slip back" even if it took constant and repeated monitoring and effort to show that he meant it.

---

[25] Likert, *New Patterns of Management*, p. 14.

[26] Hersey and Blanchard, *Management of Organizational Behavior*, 4th ed., Chapter 7.

[27] Likert, *The Human Organization*.

The first requests made to the division for capital expenditures were for improvements in the general working conditions for the hourly workers. The cafeteria, for example, was poorly lighted, poorly ventilated, and "furnished with old wire ice cream parlor chairs with paper seats and tables that were obsolete." Funds were appropriated to refurnish it and to install new lights and air conditioning. New clothes lockers were installed in areas more covenient to the men. Parking areas were expanded. A number of exhaust fans were installed. Large heaters were brought in to compensate for cold drafts at the rail freight doors. Electric fans were installed in the areas that were particularly hot in the summer. The entire receiving area was relocated to eliminate the cold drafts and to facilitate more rapid unloading. Elevator platforms were put in to eliminate hand loading. The plant hospital was air conditioned. The washrooms were repainted and then later tiled. New plumbing was installed.

A union officer commented on some of these changes as follows:

> We could see that Cooley meant business. And he fixed up the toilets in the paint shop. This didn't make much impression on the men, and they still didn't take care of them, but management kept fixing them up. The other manager simply said that the company would not fix them up. Cooley kept asking the union all the time for suggestions as to how they could be kept clean. He would always drop in on our committee meetings to get suggestions on these changes or to tell us first thing when he heard word that requests were approved. He did this on all the big plans or changes in policy.

Once the hygiene factors were beginning to improve and the dissatisfiers were being eliminated, plans could be made to improve some of the areas of potential satisfaction (motivators) related to the work itself. [28]

This clearly illustrates the influence the economic/technical system can have on the human/social system. The problems that earlier appeared on the surface to be interpersonal were solved eventually by change in the economic/technical system and the plant layout and work flow. As technical operations became more efficient, the human system also became more effective.

This also supports Guest's earlier comment about the origins of **human** *conflict resulting from* **technological** *malfunctions. Now we are beginning to see a change in the sociotechnical cycle with positive and mutually reinforcing effects of both "social" and "technical" changes.*

---

[28] Herzberg, *Work and the Nature of Man.*

Bales[29] *found in his small-group research that often two leaders emerge—one concentrates on getting the task done while the other deals with the socioemotional dynamics in the group. Litterer*[30] *hypothesizes that a single individual is under a certain amount of strain when he or she attempts to play both roles simultaneously. To the extent that Cooley set forward the broad goals to be achieved, he was a task leader. But it was the production manager, however, who acted as the day-to-day taskmaster. Why was his "rough and tough" behavior not resented, one might ask? The answer is obvious from the case, "he was accelerating the kinds of changes everyone agreed were needed."*

In examining the profiles from thousands of LEAD (Leader Effectiveness and Adaptability Description) Instruments,[31] *Hersey and Blanchard have found some interesting results. They have some implications for the different leadership styles used by Cooley and the production manager. The LEAD, an outgrowth of Situational Leadership Theory, measures three aspects of leadership: (1) style, (2) style range (flexibility), and (3) style adaptability (effectiveness). LEAD profiles reveal that managers in all kinds of organizations tend to be seen basically as using one of the task or relationship styles. Few leaders reveal significant flexibility to use all four of the leadership styles described in Situational Leadership Theory—high task/low relationship; high task/ high relationship; high relationship/low task; and low relationship/low task. Thus, since style flexibility is not widespread, Hersey and Blanchard*[32]

---

[29] R. F. Bales, "Task Roles and Social Roles in Problem-Solving Groups" in Maccoby, et al., *Readings in Social Psychology,* 3rd ed. (New York: Holt, Rinehart & Winston, 1958), pp. 437–47.

[30] Joseph A. Litterer, *The Analysis of Organizations,* 2nd ed. (New York: John Wiley and Sons, Inc., 1973), p. 175.

[31] The development of LEAD (formerly known as the Leader Adaptability and Style Inventory, LASI) is based on the theoretical frameworks presented in Hersey and Blanchard, *Management of Organizational Behavior.* 4th ed. The first article on LEAD, "So You Want to Know Your Leadership Style?" appeared in the *Training and Development Journal* (February 1974). For a detailed discussion of LEAD profiles, see *Management of Organizational Behavior,* Chapter 11.

[32] Hersey and Blanchard, *Management of Organizational Behavior,* 4th ed., Chapters 6 and 9.

THE PLANT Y CASE

CASE

The production manager in the early part of the Cooley administration played an important role in the change efforts. He was known as a "no-nonsense" type of boss with a thorough knowledge of plant operations. He was constantly out on the shop floor lending his expertise and authority in solving the technical bottlenecks. His personal behavior, unlike that of Cooley, was described as "rough and tough," but he was accepted by supervisors because he was accelerating the kinds of changes everyone agreed were needed.

argue that one way to expand one's range of behavior is through team building—working with people who supplement rather than replicate one's leadership style. Cooley (a high task/high relationship "selling" and a high relationship/low task "participating" leader) did this with his production manager (a high task/low relationship "telling" leader).

For two managers with different styles, such as Cooley and the production manager, to work together and not get into a personality conflict, it was necessary that they have **shared expectations.**[33] *That is, they had to understand and appreciate the need for each other's role and they had to have the same goals.*

In the beginning, interactions were originated almost entirely by top managers. Once the interactions were initiated, however, lower level supervisors were urged to "freewheel" on problems that they thought needed attention. As Guest points out, "Here was a significant shift in the content of interactions between managers and subordinates. Subordinates perceived the manager's conversations not as preludes to directives by the manager, as had been the case before, but as informal means for them to comment on problems and solutions as seen by the subordinates."[34]

This is evidence of the different but mutually supportive roles played by the plant manager and his production manager.

---

[33] Ibid.
[34] Guest, *Organizational Change*, p. 109.

92

The sequence of events leading to the physical changes is illustrated by the remarks of one of the general foremen. He described how the plant manager and production manager had first come around and asked foremen and general foremen for suggestions on how operations in the trim department could be improved. Later, according to the general foreman, his superintendent began to hold meetings with foremen and general foremen to discuss and agree upon a minimum number of changes. Next, the production manager took over a further series of meetings, which included members of the service as well as production groups. As the general foreman observed:

> *The material people and us had our differences of opinion, but we thrashed it all out, and there was a good spirit about it. We finally arrived at something to satisfy all of us. We felt that they must have meant business this time because the okay came from the plant manager. Then the production manager would barrel it through.*

The same pattern of group action could be observed in the physical changes made in other sections of the plant.

Because the sense of emergency had been removed from Plant Y and people were beginning to behave in mature, responsible ways, managers at every level were able to shift emphasis from controlling the behavior of the people they were responsible for (subordinates) to spending more time planning and working with the people they were responsible to (superiors). Playing this "linking pin role" (Likert[35]) gave people the opportunity to spend more time in problem solving, long-range planning, and coordinating their group's activities with the activities of other groups.

Greiner[36] argues that growing organizations move through five relatively calm periods of **evolution** *(creativity, direction, delegation, coordination, and collaboration), each of which ends with a period of crisis and* **revolution** *(crisis of leadership, autonomy, control, and red tape). According to Greiner, each evolutionary period is characterized by the dominant* **management style** *used to achieve growth, while each revolutionary period is characterized by the dominant* **management problem** *that must be solved before growth will continue.[37] Under the directive leadership of Stewart and top management, the growth of Plant Y was being disrupted by the second revolutionary stage—the crisis of autonomy (managers were stifled from taking initiative on their own). It is interesting to note how Cooley not only overcomes the crisis of autonomy but seems to avert the crisis of control and red tape by moving through the various evolutionary periods more consistent with the sequencing that Situational Leadership Theory would suggest—direction to coordination to collaboration to delegation—than the ordering depicted by Greiner—direction to delegation, back to coordination, then to collaboration.*

Again, as the annoyances in the technical systems were eliminated, the interpersonal relations began to improve.

---

[35] Likert, *New Patterns of Management.*

[36] Larry E. Greiner, "Evaluation and Revolution as Organizations Grow," *Harvard Business Review,* July–August 1972, pp. 37–46.

[37] Ibid., p. 40.

A corollary effect of the physical changes was to eliminate, so supervision reported, the extreme sense of emergency. Many comments were similar to those of the general foreman who said:

> *With all those little changes and big changes, we have more time to get around. And with more time we can think a little bit more about planning, instead of worrying what's going to happen the next minute. This may sound like small stuff, and I suppose if you take any one of the changes it probably is a small thing, but if you work out in the shop, you can see these small things are important. As they kept making different changes, these small changes had a way of snowballing. Each one gives us that much more chance to think ahead so that we don't get into a hole the next time. Also, it was when the men saw some of these changes being made that they began to believe that we were trying to do something for them. You can talk a lot about human relations, but unless you can show something that you have done, why it is only a lot of talk. We used to get that talk in the old training sessions, but it didn't mean anything.*

Implicit in this comment and in others like it is that change was not sudden and dramatic but was rather the product of many small changes. The improvements in operations gave supervision more time to plan and reduce the potential for interpersonal conflict. As one foreman put it:

> *It ain't perfect, but we're getting some place. It seems like every single section foreman on the line is trying to run his section the best way he can for the whole line. All of us are more willing to get along because there are fewer reasons for squawking at each other.*

The establishment of various types of regularly scheduled meetings, according to Guest,[38] helped Cooley "institutionalize" a new sentiment-interaction pattern. These meetings were new activities that resulted in two-way or multiway interactions. People became involved at all levels. Positive sentiments developed from these meetings because those participating gained further assurance that the new manager was not using and did not intend to use autocratic ("telling") measures to gain acceptance. Participants freely expressed ideas and suggestions not only to the plant manager but, what is perhaps even more important, to one another. The meetings introduced a new form of lateral or peer interaction among those in the higher echelons, which was sustained not in the meetings alone but in day-to-day relationships. Thus, one segment of the total organization—members at higher levels—had within the first few months adopted a pattern that later spread to all levels of the managerial group.

Cooley was establishing mechanisms for feedback and short-term goal setting. People could get a sense of how well they were doing and where they were headed next. Under Stewart the environment was dominated by punishment and negative reinforcement. What Cooley, in essence, was doing was setting up a systematic **positive reinforcement** schedule where he was able to reward improved behavior as soon as possible. This is similar to a behavior modification[39] concept called **reinforcing positively successive approximations of a desired behavior.** This is an important concept because when an organization's performance has been declining over a period of time, as was the case with Plant Y, one cannot expect drastic changes overnight. The effective manager uses positive reinforcement as the behavior approaches the desired level of

---

[38] Much of this discussion is taken from Guest, *Organizational Change*, pp. 110–11.

[39] The most classic discussions of behavior modification, reinforcement theory, or operant conditioning have been done by B. F. Skinner; see his *Science and Human Behavior* (New York: The MacMillan Company, 1953). See also, A. Bandura, *Principles of Behavior Modification* (New York: Holt, Rinehart, & Winston, 1969), and C. M. Franks, *Behavior Therapy: Appraisal and Status* (New York: McGraw-Hill Book Company, 1969).

III. INTRODUCTION OF MEETINGS

During the months following Cooley's succession to office, he established a series of regularly scheduled meetings, which in time directly or indirectly involved members of supervision at all levels. These continued for the balance of his three-year term of office.

The scope and function of the meetings established by the new manager stood in marked contrast to those of the earlier period: there were more of them, they were regularly scheduled, they covered a wider range of activities, more people took part in them, and they were oriented not only to the present but to the long-range future.

The most general type of meeting was held once every month in the plant cafeteria and attended by all members of the plant supervision. Its essential purpose, according to the manager, was "to tell everyone in the organization what was ahead for the next 30 days, review the past 30 days, and answer questions that came up." Supervisors were encouraged to submit written questions about any subject. The manager promised frank answers.

Once each week a meeting was held that included the plant manager and those reporting directly to him—his immediate staff. These meetings were concerned with new developments, information, and directives stemming from the division and corporation. "Cooley was also interested in us as people, our jobs, what those below us wanted and needed—how the whole show could be put together."

performance. Managers must be **aware** *of any progress of subordinates so that they will be in a position to reinforce this change appropriately. This strategy is compatible with the concept of setting interim rather than final performance criteria and then rewarding the subordinate as interim goals are accomplished. Such systematic goal setting and feedback were characteristic of Cooley's style.*

These meetings demonstrated that Cooley was not going to use the "autocratic" decision-making style that characterized Stewart's management. Rather he was going to use "consultative" and "group" decision-making styles (Vroom and Yetton). In using a group style, a leader not only shares problems with subordinates and evaluates alternatives with group members, but also works to a consensus on solutions without dictating his or her own solution.[40]

---

[40]Vroom and Yetton, *Leadership and Decision Making.*

Also once each week a cost meeting was held by the comptroller and production manager with the plant manager present.
Included were the heads of the personnel and work standards
departments and all supervisors in the production organization
down through the level of general foremen. The comptroller
presented the current figures on costs and plant efficiency; the
production manager made comments interpreting these figures.
Questions and suggestions were put forward by the participants.

This same group, with the addition of the chief inspector,
met once a week to review matters relating to inspection and
quality.

The director of material control met with all of his salaried
employees, including material control clerks. These meetings
were often followed by sessions with the hourly wage stock handlers.

Lower level managers were beginning to identify with and model Cooley's behavior. Now that the unfreezing (Lewin[41]) was done and people seemed to be motivated to change, Cooley could move to the changing phase. During this phase a manager can use one or more of Kelman's three mechanisms for change—compliance, identification, and internalization.[42]

Since Cooley seemed to be using a participative change cycle,[43] compliance was not used as a mechanism for change. Instead, he combined identification and internalization into an effective strategy for change. Cooley "set the pattern" for the organization through his behavior. He reinforced a willingness to consider alternative points of view and a dedication to organizational goals. Having established a model that he "meant what he said" about making changes, he prepared managers psychologically to respond favorably and begin to internalize new patterns of behavior, which were slowly permeating down from above.

Internalization, in particular, began to take place as need levels turned from physiological and safety/security to affiliation and esteem needs (Maslow[44]). As Homans[45] would predict: new "activities" (the meetings) stepped up the frequency of "interactions," which led not only to positive feelings ("sentiments") about getting the job done but also to feelings of camaraderie as an emergent value "in itself."

This is tangible proof that Cooley's early statement—"I don't believe in firing a lot of people and using threats and fear"—was not just words.

---

[41] Lewin, "Frontiers in Group Dynamics."

[42] H. C. Kelman, "Compliance, Identification and Internationization: Three Processes of Attitude Change," *Conflict Resolutions,* II (1958), 51–60.

[43] Hersey and Blanchard, *Management of Organizational Behavior,* 4th ed., Chapter 10.

[44] Maslow, *Motivation and Personality.*

[45] Homans, *The Human Group.*

THE PLANT Y CASE

Within four months it was observed that operating and service departments at lower levels were also beginning to meet. There is no indication that these meetings were specifically ordered by Matt Cooley or his immediate subordinates. As a staff person said, "They just seemed to happen. It was working for others and could work for us. Things were opening up and we had a lot of ideas we wanted to talk about."

Several members of supervision at first thought that group meetings were too "time consuming." But, as a general foreman put it, "it began to dawn on us that if we ever were to stop running around and putting out fires, we had to do this. Also, just getting together as a group was worth something in itself."

IV. SHIFTS IN PERSONNEL

Plant Y experienced many shifts in supervisory personnel. However, no more than three of the 300 salaried personnel were discharged or asked to resign during the next two years. (Under the previous manager more than 40 supervisors were fired or demoted in one year.)

The manager is adopting Miles's **human resources** *leadership model in his efforts continually to expand his subordinates' responsibility and self-direction up to the limits of their ability and desires. Miles rejects the earlier simplistic assumptions of the* **human relations** *model, the primary objective being simply to increase the morale and satisfaction of subordinates.*[46]

Many organizations promote managers only on the basis of their performance (productivity). Less used is another criterion for promotion— "having a ready replacement." By encouraging supervisors to develop understudies, Cooley was reinforcing their use of high relationship/low task ("participating") and low relationship/low task ("delegating") styles. Both these styles, according to Situational Leadership Theory, would be appropriate for subordinates of moderate to high levels of task-relevant maturity. Yet as Hersey and Blanchard[47] have found in examining data from their LEAD instrument, the "delegating" style is probably the least used. However, it is essential if one is to develop subordinates capable of "taking over" when the time comes.

---

[46]Raymond E. Miles, "Human Relations or Human Resources," *Harvard Business Review,* July–August 1965.

[47]Hersey and Blanchard, *Management of Organizational Behavior,* 4th ed., Chapter 9.

THE PLANT Y CASE

Cooley did bring in a new production manager; another plant had requested the former production manager. Several foremen, general foremen, and three superintendents who were on temporary assignment at Plant Y returned to their "home" plants during the first year. They were not replaced by "outsiders"; their jobs were filled by persons within Plant Y itself.

The shifts in job assignments took many forms. An inspection foreman, for example, was transferred to the material control department and later was placed in charge of inspection for the entire plant. A foreman on the shipping line became number two man in material control. A production foreman in the metal department was moved over to the trim department, where he later became shift superintendent, then department superintendent.

The promotions were made possible for two reasons: (1) the vacancies that occurred when several members of supervision returned to their "home" plants, and (2) the vacancies that occurred when other plants requested some supervisors from Plant Y. (In this latter connection, Plant Y in time came to be looked upon as a "training ground" for other plants.)

Every supervisor in the organization was encouraged to develop understudies. A deliberate long-range program was instituted in which each member of management above the foreman level in the line and service departments gave his job over to one or more of his subordinates for a temporary period of sixty days.

A *participative change cycle*[48] *begins when people are given new knowledge. Cooley was providing managers with cognitive input that would lead to increased commitment to organizational goals, bolster the technical competence of individuals/groups, and help to minimize intergroup conflict.*

By shifting people into other positions, Cooley began to enlarge people's "span of cognition," in Guest's terms[49]—*that is, to provide them with a greater awareness of, knowledge about, and interest in the role others were performing, and how these roles "fit together" in the total organization.*

These transfers also insured internalization (Kelman[50]*) of new attitudes and behaviors. As Schein contends, if new behavior has been internalized while being learned, "this has automatically facilitated refreezing because it has been fitted naturally into the individual's personality."*[51]

Here is an illustration of how Cooley used positive reinforcement rather than punishment.

---

[48] Ibid.

[49] Guest, *Organizational Change*, pp. 130–31.

[50] Kelman, "Compliance, Identification."

[51] Edgar H. Schein, "Management Development as a Process of Influence," in *Behavioral Concepts in Management*, ed. David H. Hampton (Belmont, Calif.: Dickenson Publishing Co., Inc., 1968), p. 110. Reprinted from *Industrial Management Review* (May 1961), 59–77.

THE PLANT Y CASE

Initially, it took some time for men transferred to become familiar with the new operations and a new group of subordinates. In the long run, their knowledge of many aspects of plant operations was expanded. As one foreman observed:

> *The thing we have noticed is that they do move the foremen around a lot more than they ever did before. I think it is helpful because it gives the foreman a much broader knowledge of the job. Before, we used to scream at each other like a bunch of washerwomen, and that was mostly out of ignorance. Now, when some of the foremen go into some of the sections where they were before, they have a better appreciation of what their old problem was like.*

Transfers were not made in large numbers at one time. The method was to pinpoint specific areas in order of priority and to "try out" a man for a period of time. If he did not "work out," he was not discharged but returned to the job he knew better.

ANALYSIS

Since Cooley's arrival, Plant Y had moved from a survival crisis mentality, where security was the predominant need, to a satisfaction of security and safety needs and finally to where people now finally were most interested in recognition and self-actualization (Maslow[1]).

Cooley had broken the ineffective cycle created by Stewart. As Hersey and Blanchard would contend, now the effective cycle was in operation—that is, supervisors and managers at all levels were responding well to Cooley's high expectations and trust in them. They were performing well; this reinforced Cooley's high expectations and produced even higher performance.[2] It became an upward spiraling effect because of the increased leverage created through the use of motivators (Herzberg[3]).

It is important to note that "turning the ship around" did not happen overnight simply by Cooley replacing Stewart's low expectations with his own high expectations. The key to Cooley's strategy, as discussed earlier, was his tendency to reinforce positively "interim behavior" of managers as they approached a desired level of performance. For example, with modest Plant Y performance improvements, Cooley sought—and received—more division support for technical improvements. By actually instituting changes that various project groups had decided upon, Cooley reinforced their self-confidence and willingness to contribute.

---

[1]Abraham H. Maslow, *Motivation and Personality* (New York: Harper and Row, Publishers, 1954).

[2]Paul Hersey and Kenneth H. Blanchard, *Management of Organizational Behavior,* 4th ed. (Englewood Cliffs, N.J.: Prentice-Hall, Inc., 1982), Chapter 6.

[3]Frederick Herzberg, *Work and the Nature of Man* (New York: World Publishing Co., 1966).

I. TURNING THINGS AROUND—A SLOW PROCESS

For several months Plant Y's performance indices showed little change. Then, one by one, there were small signs of improvement. Inspection reports began to show positive changes. Grievances were decreasing, as were direct and indirect labor costs. These signs of change served as proof to everyone, so they reported, that Plant Y was actually capable of changing. Positive results served to reinforce the confidence of supervision in itself. By the end of eighteen months plant personnel were no longer satisfied with having moved up somewhat from bottom position in their comparative standing with other plants. They "had tasted blood," as one observer put it, and nothing short of being *first* among the six sister plants would satisfy them. In thirty months, as the figures later show, Plant Y reached this goal in most performance indices.

The members of Plant Y were now able to stand back and view the reality of change in a rational manner. Under Stewart, they had been in the midst of conflict and confusion, unable to reflect. Indeed, they did not have time to reflect upon what was really happening to them, other than the fact that they were "in a mess." Now they had time to put things in perspective.

These comments support the argument that the plant before Cooley arrived had supervisory personnel who were able and had sufficient education and experience to be competent managers. But because of the "climate of fear," they were not willing (motivated) to take responsibility or set high but obtainable goals (achievement motivation). Thus, although these supervisors had the potential for moderate maturity (Hersey/

Looking back at their experience over three years, members of management at all levels took pride in comparing present success with former conditions. One superintendent observed:

> *A lot of people apparently think that this plant was not a successful plant in the old days. I don't think this is quite true. There were times when this plant was not too bad. But all I can say is that success, whatever we had of success, was paid for at a great cost. What a cost! How was it done? Out-and-out fear. This plant ran on fear and fear alone. Get me straight now. We still have intense competition with the other plants, and in a way that's a kind of fear, but nobody who knows he's doing a reasonably good job has any fear of losing his job. Fear in the old days was based on the simple principle, "If you can't do it, get out."*

The expressed sense of release was revealed in other ways. Supervisors often observed that ideas for improving the organization had long existed in their minds, but that these ideas could not be expressed because of the prevailing "climate of fear." One superintendent put it:

> *What happened around here, as I see it, is that what they have tried to do is to formalize in a program many of the things which the best supervisors did in the first place. The trouble was in the old days that what some of the best foremen did was often frowned upon. Today we operate in the open and do many of the things that we used to have to hide.*

Blanchard[4]), they were forced to behave in passive, dependent, subordinate ways (Argyris[5]).

When the decision was made to replace the earlier plant manager, we raised the question as to whether Stewart could have turned the situation around if he had suddenly changed his behavior and started to behave in ways that employees thought were legitimate. In response to that question, we suggested that the probability was low that Stewart could reverse the downward spiraling productivity and morale because of the large reservoir of negative past experience the personnel in Plant Y had had with him. Any change in his behavior would have had little impact on their basic negative feelings and expectations (developed over time) about the way that he had behaved. In fact, they would probably be waiting for the return of his "real self." The same phenomenon seems

---

[4]Hersey and Blanchard, *Management of Organizational Behavior*, 4th ed., Chapter 7.

[5]Chris Argyris, *Personality and Organization* (New York: Harper and Row, Publishers, 1957), and *Integrating the Individual and the Organization* (New York: John Wiley and Sons, Inc., 1964).

A general foreman drew the contrast:

> *Before things changed, I had just about reached a point of thinking that all the things I believed in were wrong. I had always believed that if you treat people right, you will be treated the right way.*
>
> *I was under the impression that this was the way to operate. But then I began to believe that my whole thinking was wrong and that I should pattern myself after the way the people on top operated. I couldn't resolve this conflict within myself and started to make inquiries about a job outside. (laugh) Now I'm convinced that I was dead right, because that's just the way we are operating in this organization from the top down now.*

This comment as well as many others leaves the impression that Cooley never "applied pressure" and that he always consulted with subordinates before making any decisions. This was not so. There were many instances during his administration when Cooley had to act in what appeared to be an arbitrary manner. Sudden decisions related to schedule changes and other important matters affecting all plants were made at division and corporate levels and transmitted to the plants for immediate implementation. Or within Plant Y itself an occasional emergency would come up requiring direct orders from Cooley with no opportunity for staff discussion. Cooley would issue an order and expect immediate unquestioned compliance. He was behaving, in short, in a manner that on the surface appeared to be uncharacteristic of the Matt Cooley described throughout the Plant Y story. How his people reacted to such "arbitrary behavior" is best explained in a comment of one of the general foremen:

to have happened here with Cooley but in a positive direction. The fact that Cooley had built up a history or reservoir of positive supportive behavior permitted him to behave occasionally in very different ways without affecting the overall feelings the Plant Y personnel had about him. Thus, whenever Cooley applied pressure or acted firmly without involving others, he was trusted. There was a good reason. It did not signal a **general** *change in his managerial behavior.*

The removal of pressure and "interference from above" changed another significant causal variable (Likert[6]) in the Plant Y environment—the style and expectations of the higher management. When production in Plant Y began to decline, Stewart's superiors expected him to get productivity back on the upswing. These expectations seemed to force Stewart to operate in a crisis-oriented, autocratic way. However, when Cooley was given charge as plant manager, a "hands off" policy was initiated by his superiors. The fact that the expectations of top management had changed enough to put a moratorium on random, troublesome outside stimuli from headquarters gave Cooley an opportunity to operate in a completely different style.[7]

---

[6]Rensis Likert, *The Human Organization* (New York: McGraw-Hill Book Company, 1967).

[7]Hersey and Blanchard, *Management of Organizational Behavior,* 4th ed., Chapter 6.

THE PLANT Y CASE

There are times when we get orders from the front office to suddenly shift away from what we thought had been agreed upon and we would not complain. Let me explain it this way. Good human relations is like money in the savings account. If you don't put any money away you can't draw any out when you need it. Matt Cooley was putting money in this account from the day he arrived. Occasionally an emergency would come up and he would have to lower the boom with no questions asked. When he did this he was drawing some money out of the account. He got away with it because we trusted him. We knew there was a good reason, and, as you would expect, he would explain later why he did it. The fellow we had before (Stewart) never had any reserves to draw on. There's a big difference.

II. PLANT Y RELATIONSHIP TO THE DIVISION

One significant change was not in the organization itself but in its relationship to the division. From the day of the new manager's arrival, there was an abrupt reduction of "interference from above." Standard directives, notices, and information of the kind all plants received continued, but specific directives—ordering the manager at Plant Y what to do in response to each administrative crisis—came to a halt. Cooley was given some breathing space to "show what he could do." Top management had given him a blank check. They said to him, in effect, "We don't care what you do as long as you get the plant out of the mess it is in." This is what Cooley "heard," and he took full advantage of it.

ANALYSIS

As Guest argues, only when a leader is granted "leeway to act" by his superiors "can he (1) set realistic goals or targets which both he and his subordinates can meet through collaborative effort, (2) openly acknowledge interdependence, and (3) integrate the productive requirements of the total organization with the immediate needs of subordinates."[8]

Also, permission to act without constant dictation by superiors makes it easier for the leader to play the dual "linking pin" role (Likert[9]) both as an agent of high authorities and as representative of his organization to higher authorities without letting one role dominate the other as Stewart did.

It should be emphasized here that it was a risk for the executive vice-president to say "let Cooley alone" when his first six months of leadership provided no tangible (output/productivity) evidence of progress. Yet, it was important that he took that stand and seemingly realized that it takes time to make significant change and turn an organization around, especially one that had been in a downward spiraling condition in terms of both productivity and the condition of its human resources (intervening variables[10]). By taking the pressure off, top management was permitting Cooley and his managers time to react to contingencies as a challenge rather than a crisis. As a result, management was able to operate more from a rational, problem-solving adult ego state rather than from emotional child or evaluative parent ego states (Berne[11]).

---

[8]Robert H. Guest, *Organizational Change: The Effect of Successful Leadership* (Homewood, Ill.: The Dorsey Press, Inc. and Richard D. Irwin, Inc., 1962), p. 128.
[9]Rensis Likert, *New Patterns of Management* (New York: McGraw-Hill Book Company, 1961).
[10]Likert, *The Human Organization.*
[11]Eric Berne, *Games People Play* (New York: Grove Press, Inc., 1964).

THE PLANT Y CASE

One incident is significant. Six months after Cooley took over, a group of top corporate executives were discussing Plant Y's progress at lunch in the corporate executive dining room in Michigan. The division manager made a comment indicating his concern that Plant Y showed little if any improvement and that perhaps he, the division manager, should do something about it. The executive vice-president in charge of all corporate production operations turned to the division manager with the terse comment, "Let Cooley alone."

More evidence of the identification model (Kelman[12]) that Cooley played in the change process and his belief in Theory Y assumptions about human nature (McGregor[13]).

Cooley "down played" his **position power** and acted to influence people more with his **personal power** (Etzioni[14]).

Plant Y seems to be operating now with humanistic/democratic organizational values with a YB top manager. Trusting, authentic relationships are developing, which should result in increased interpersonal competence, intergroup cooperation, and organizational effectiveness (Argyris[15]).

---

[12]H. C. Kelman, "Compliance, Identification and Internalization: Three Processes of Attitude Change," *Conflict Resolutions*, II (1958), 51–60.

[13]Douglas McGregor, *The Human Side of Enterprise* (New York: McGraw-Hill Book Company, 1960).

[14]Amitai Etzioni, *A Comparative Analysis of Complex Organizations* (New York: The Free Press, 1961).

[15]Chris Argyris, "Interpersonal Barriers to Decision Making," *Harvard Business Review* (22), 2:84–97, 1966, and *Interpersonal Competence and Organizational Effectiveness* (Homewood, Ill.: The Dorsey Press, Inc. and Richard D. Irwin, Inc., 1962). See also, *Management and Organizational Development: The Path From XA to YB* (New York: McGraw-Hill Book Company, 1971).

III. THE PLANT MANAGER'S ROLE
IN THE PROCESS OF CHANGE

Within Plant Y itself, several supervisors described how Cooley's behavior "set the pattern" for the entire organization. A general foreman remarked, "It's just the general approach he had toward everything, and it goes right down through the organization." A foreman added: "He feels that a fellow is an individual and you have to treat him as an individual, and he means it."

The way in which members of supervision regarded Cooley's informal visits and conversations with foremen on the shop floor stood in sharp contrast to their opinions of similar activities of Stewart, the plant manager in the earlier period. Now they regarded these face-to-face contacts as a means of exchanging technical ideas or of "socializing" and not for the purpose of punishment. Cooley avoided, in his words and in his dress, any display of superior status. Here are some typical random comments of foremen:

> *What a difference! Like night and day. The manager comes down and jokes a lot. That's something we never had before.*
>
> *This plant has improved 100 percent, and I think it's mostly the manager. He walks around the plant and talks with the men. He just wears an old beat-up jacket and doesn't act superior.*
>
> *The manager goes all over the plant and speaks to everybody. Not the way it used to be. He comes up and says "good morning" to me and the men, and he means it.*
>
> *The foremen all know he is pulling for the foremen and has a lot of respect for the foremen's judgement.*

Now that hygiene factors (Herzberg[16]), such as job security, working conditions, supervision, and interpersonal relations and lower level security and social needs (Maslow[17]), are well satisfied, the "motivator" factors, such as recognition for accomplishment, increased responsibility, upper level esteem, and self-actualization needs, are manifest.

As discussed earlier, it did not take long for supervision at Plant Y to accept Cooley soon after he took over. He began with a "clean slate." Few had known him before. They liked what they heard. It took much longer, however, for more than three hundred members of management down five levels of the hierarchy to reflect the change in their own day-to-day behavior. It took thousands of small "reinforcing" incidents for them to "feel" the change. (See also earlier observations about positive reinforcement.)

---

[16]Herzberg, *Work and the Nature of Man*.
[17]Maslow, *Motivation and Personality*.

The Plant Y Case

> *The foreman knows that if he's got the stuff, he's going to be recognized and promoted. He knows top management wants to help the foremen get ahead.*

This "promotion" theme was mentioned often after the change. Earlier, the emphasis was on job survival alone. No one expressed the hope of advancing in the organization; no one expressed even the desire to advance.

IV. CHANGES IN VERTICAL RELATIONSHIPS BELOW THE PLANT MANAGER

Supervision often made a distinction between the swift change in attitudes toward one person—the plant manager—following his succession to office, and the slow change in attitudes toward or perceptions about their immediate superiors, subordinates, and peers. They indicated that they had to go through many experiences—successful experiences in solving technical problems—before fear and distrust of the intentions of their superiors could be eliminated. A general foreman expressed it this way:

> *It's hard to explain the reason for what has happened. There was no sudden overturn. Just gradually we learned how to do the job, how to take care of things one at a time. In an outfit like this you can change the speed of the conveyor by pushing a couple of buttons, but you can't do that with people. It's like a kid riding a bike. He has to do it time and time again before he gets the hang of it. I had to feel that those above me were trying to act a little more human. It's been a great improvement.*

As **sentiments** *became more positive, they resulted in an environment where* **interactions** *and communication flow accelerated in all directions (Homans[18]).*

In addition to improvements in the human skills, managers began to be concerned about conceptual skills (Katz[19])—not only wanting to do their job right but being concerned about how it fit into the total organization.

The environment now was characterized by positive reinforcement rather than punishment (Skinner[20]). This resulted in many more people having "I'm OK, you're OK" attitudes (Harris[21]), who were willing to engage in rational problem solving.

---

[18]George C. Homans, *The Human Group* (New York: Harcourt, Brace and Company, 1950).

[19]Robert L. Katz, "Skills of an Effective Administrator," *Harvard Business Review* (January–February 1955), pp. 33–42.

[20]B. F. Skinner, *Science and Human Behavior* (New York: The Macmillan Company, 1953).

[21]Thomas Harris, *I'm OK—You're OK: A Practical Guide to Transactional Analysis* (New York: Harper and Row, Publishers, 1969).

Regarding the change that occurred below the manager level, three observations can be made. The expressed opinions of superiors and subordinates toward each other were now more positive and favorable than they had been before. A greater amount of information was flowing upward from subordinates to superior; subordinates said that they had "easier access" to superiors. A greater proportion of communications concerned future planning rather than present emergencies.

Stressing the change from "punitive" to "rewarding" behavior, a foreman made this typical comment:

> *The general foreman will now come up when there is a problem with a man and ask you whether the man has been shown just what his job does to other operations. He checks to find out whether the man has his tools and everything he needs. Only after some exploring to make sure that I've done all I could in my power does he attempt to make a decision. He will help the foreman to decide what further action to take. This may take time, but I think it pays off. The general foreman is taking more time.*

Foremen believed that general foremen and superintendents were now helpful in solving technical problems by concentrating on the problem rather than on fixing blame on the foremen. As one foremen said:

> *When there is trouble, their attitude is to find out what the problem is first. They don't take it out on the men or the foremen as the scapegoat, but they take it out on the problem first. There are some people around here who I used to think were real bastards, but they have changed quite a lot.*

Supervisors at all levels were now starting to internalize the high relationship behavior that Cooley was modeling. This gave subordinates opportunities to start directing and controlling their own behavior. The higher expectations that people began to have for their subordinates were resulting in higher performance (self-fulfilling prophecy). This did not happen overnight, but it was a result of the continual development of people through a gradual shift from the high task/low relationship ("telling") style of Stewart to the initial high task/high relationship ("selling") style that Cooley modeled to a more high relationship/low task ("participating") style. This developmental approach matured people and prepared them for the time when they would be left more on their own (low relationship/low task) and delegated significant responsibility (Hersey and Blanchard[22]).

These foremen were suggesting that some of the managers were XB—that is, they went along with the new participative B behavior that Cooley modeled without changing their negative Theory X assumptions about human nature (McGregor[23]). If things ever reverted back to the old autocratic structured A behavior of Stewart, these foremen thought that some managers would probably revert back to XA (Argyris[24]).

---

[22] Hersey and Blanchard, *Management of Organizational Behavior*, 4th ed., Chapter 7.

[23] McGregor, *The Human Side of Enterprise*.

[24] Chris Argyris, *Management and Organizational Development*.

Foremen often observed that with additional information and help from superiors they were in a better position to make their own decisions without interference from above. In turn, they now began to trust their own subordinates to manage with a minimum of interference from them.

One of the general foremen, after recalling that formerly "I insisted that the foremen make no moves without consulting me," said:

> *Now I don't worry all the time about my foremen getting me into hot water. They have the kind of information which allows them to see beyond the next minute or the next hour. My job is to help them get what they need. I'm not as rushed, so I can spend more time listening to what they have to say. The more I do this, the more I realize what good men they really are when they have half a chance to do a job.*

Despite the greater degree of communication and trust, two of the twenty-five foremen interviewed still expressed concern about their relationship to their immediate superiors or to the superintendents. They feared that if it were not for the pattern set by Cooley as plant manager, some members of middle management would return to their former tactics of using threats or punishment. As one foreman put it: "Some of them act like they are just willing to go along, but if there should be a change in top management, they could slide right back into their old ways. That old horsewhip attitude is still underneath with some people, but they manage to hide it."

This attitudinal response again reinforces the importance of Guest's sociotechnical cycle theory.[25] *As barriers to intergroup conflict were removed, it became increasingly possible for its members to deal with technical problems in a rational manner. This is further supported by Strauss's observations about the* **work** *flow and lateral relationships in organizations with peers or members of other departments. Strauss's research*[26] *points out the importance of a smooth lateral flow of materials and operations and how it can have an effect on and be affected by lateral communications and interactions.*

---

[25]Guest, *Organizational Change,* Chapter 9.

[26]George Strauss, "Tactics of Lateral Relationship: The Purchasing Agent," *Administrative Science Quarterly,* 7, No. 2, September 1962, 161–86.

A change in reciprocal attitudes of superiors and subordinates in the production organization was paralleled by a marked change in peer relations. At all levels, people continued to meet both regularly and informally and to notify each other about potential interdepartmental problems. The foremen were affected most:

> One of the best things that I feel has happened around here is the cooperation between foremen in different sections. It used to be that when a poor operation came through from another section, the other foreman's attitude was, and I know it was true with me, too, "That's his worry." Now we try to grab it and tell the foreman about it. Just yesterday, I had some stuff going through to the next foreman which wasn't too good, but I was on the spot because the operator on a particular job wasn't too good. The foreman in the next section came up to me and told me not to worry about it, and that he would have his men fix the thing up for the time being.

V. CHANGES IN LINE-STAFF RELATIONSHIPS

Relationships between the production and nonproduction groups improved even though their respective roles as set forth in formal manuals and charts remained unchanged.

In terms of the Blake, Sheppard and Mouton Model for Managing Intergroup Conflict,[27] we see here the evolution in line-staff attitudes toward conflict. The change was from the earlier "conflict is inevitable, agreement is impossible" syndrome to an attitude that "although there may be conflict, agreement is possible." Over time, the "stakes" involved in change went from low to high. Now managers at all levels were willing to engage in problem solving where there was conflict as well as a high level of agreement.

Note also that all appropriate persons in the line and staff departments were involved in problem-solving efforts. They were not limited to working with a small number of subsystems in the organization.

In comparing Stewart and Cooley, it has been observed repeatedly that Stewart acted chiefly in response to immediate emergencies, while Cooley devoted a greater part of his time to matters related to future planning. From this observation, Guest[28] hypothesizes that a leader's efforts to induce others to meet the organization's production goals will be successful to the extent that his or her activities are focused on a longer time perspective. This same hypothesis would appear to hold true for other members at different levels of the organization.[29]

---

[27]Robert R. Blake, Herbert Sheppard, and Jane Mouton, *Managing Intergroup Conflict in Industry* (Houston: Gulf Publishing Company, 1964).

[28]Guest, *Organizational Change*, p. 129.

[29]Further support for this hypothesis was gained in direct observations of each of 56 assembly line foremen for a full eight-hour day. In an analysis of more than 32,000 incidents, it was found that the foremen who had to cope with fewer "emergencies" (1) had more time for planning, and (2) were judged by others to be more successful. See Robert H. Guest, "Of Time and the Foreman," *Personnel*, 32, No. 6 (May 1956), 478–96, also F. J. Jasinki and R. H. Guest, "Redesigning the Supervisor's Job," *Factory Mangement and Maintenance*, Vol. 115, No. 12 (December 1957).

Material Control

Early in the change process, the decision was made to assign some members of the material control and the production departments "to study the material bottlenecks, especially in the trim department." These men proceeded jointly to question foremen, general foremen, and material handlers and to observe in detail the precise sequence of material and parts movement from the loading platform to the line. Their recommendations were discussed at a staff meeting and then implemented. This pattern was followed elsewhere in the plant. At each step, not only were production and material personnel informed about the plans, but the advice of others in nonoperating departments was sought. To give members of the material control department some perspective on the progress of the plans as they were put into effect, the weekly material department meetings referred to earlier were begun.

The foremen's activities with respect to material control matters shifted from having to handle emergencies to planning that would obviate emergencies. In carrying out these activities, the foremen, and indeed all members of operating supervision, talked frequently with clerks and supervisors in material control about future actions to improve the system.

This is further evidence that the decision-making method in Plant Y had moved from an autocratic style under Stewart to consultative and now group styles under Cooley (Vroom and Yetton[30]).

Stewart's authority had been less effective, Guest argues,[31] because of his exclusive reliance on the formal vertical structure of the organization. In general, information had flowed vertically through the chain of command within one of the formally designated functions (production, inspection, accounting, whatever). After decisions had been made at high levels, the information or directives would then be passed down through the separate channels of the other departments. Each group had been regarded as a distinctly separate function, much the way it would appear on the formal organizational chart. Yet technologically the organization was based upon a continuous-flow principle, which made it necessary for information to flow along horizontal planes. Any actual or potential interruption in the work flow often required simultaneous action on the part of the members of several structurally "separate" groups.

By not insisting that information on a work flow problem be transmitted up through the "proper" **and** *separate channels for decision and back down through other formal channels, Cooley in effect modified the traditional structure of organization to meet more realistically the technological requirements.*

---

[30]Victor H. Vroom and Philip Yetton, *Leadership and Decision Making* (Pittsburgh: University of Pittsburgh Press, 1973).

[31]Guest, *Organizational Change*, p. 129.

This condition resulted in a change in the way major decisions were made in the top echelons. Recommendations for action were introduced to the manager and his staff, having already been thoroughly discussed among those at lower levels. Usually a number of alternative proposals (drawn up jointly by the production and material control groups) were submitted.

Inspection

The process of change in the relationship between the two groups described above closely parallels the change occurring in production/inspection relationships. The first phase began with direct and informal conversations on the shop floor between the manager and members of both groups. Then weekly meetings instituted by Cooley were attended by the chief inspector and operating supervisors down through the general foreman level. At first these meetings were exploratory. Each participant was encouraged to spell out what he considered to be the critical problem areas involving quality. Later the group blocked out an outline of a training and informational program for operating and inspection foremen and for hourly inspectors. Details of procedure were then worked out among the training director, chief inspector, and other representatives of the operating departments. Ideas from the material control, maintenance, and work standards departments were also solicited.

Here is good evidence that the perceptions of the line personnel had changed toward staff people such as inspectors. Under Stewart, foremen had regarded the presence and actions of inspectors with suspicion and resentment. They had come to feel that inspection's role was solely to "put us on the spot." Under Cooley, however, with virtually no change in the functions of inspection as prescribed "in the manual," the roles of these groups were perceived quite differently and favorably. This supports the old concept that it is not reality that affects behavior but the way one perceives and integrates that reality.

Now that the foremen saw inspection as trying to help, they were no longer threatened. They felt that greater control was being given rather than being taken away from them, even though the standards were getting tougher.

When a representative from the work standards department had the authority to determine work assignments for production, Guest found the interactions between these two groups were "originated primarily by work standards; the response was compliance or evasion by the foreman."[32] By getting work standard's staff to accept a service as well as a

---

[32]Ibid., p. 91.

Foremen tended to emphasize three changes in the relationship. The first was that operating supervision and members of the inspection department agreed with each other as to what was acceptable quality and what was not. A second related point was that communications between operating supervision and inspection were not dominated by the inspection group. "We tip each other off." That is, under former conditions, a foreman, as one of them admitted, "might just let some stuff slip by hoping it would be missed by the inspectors and fixed up later in conditioning." In the new inspection/production relationship, the production foreman would inform inspection to keep an eye on certain kinds of jobs that were causing trouble. A third observation made by most of the foremen was the acceptance of the inspector "as part of my group." In the new relationship, foremen were encouraged to share problems with inspection. The inspector's primary function of passing on quality had not changed, but the roles that each perceived for the other had changed.

It is interesting to note that greater acceptance of inspectors took place in spite of the fact that quality standards for the entire division had measurably stiffened during the first two years of Cooley's administration.

Work Standards

The new administration recognized that the rigid controls exercised by the work standards department were resented by the foremen; here was one further source of administrative control that limited the foremen's authority. After several months of *control function, the foremen determined more frequently who was to do how much with respect to what job on the assembly line.*

With the shift from autocratic to consultative and group decision-making styles (Vroom and Yetton[33]), the power for making decisions was returned to the operating managers. As a result, the leadership style of staff personnel was limited to "selling" and "participating" (Hersey and Blanchard[34]).

According to Guest, this change, in terms of interactions (Homans[35]), "meant fewer contacts were originated by work standards and directed at production supervision, and the proportion of contacts (not necessarily the total volume) made by the foremen to the work standards representative for technical advice was higher. As in many other events involving production and nonproduction groups, discussions between operating supervision and work standards were oriented more toward the future, that is, toward planning in advance for readjustments of work loads in light of a known schedule change to come."[36]

---

[33]Vroom and Yetton, *Leadership and Decision Making.*
[34]Hersey and Blanchard, *Management of Organizational Behavior,* 4th ed., Chapter 7.
[35]Homans, *The Human Group.*
[36]Guest, *Organizational Change,* pp. 90–91.

THE PLANT Y CASE

discussions between the work standards department and operating supervision at all levels, a change in policy was made. As Cooley described it:

> The foreman was made chiefly responsible for determining the work assignment of the individual worker. Before it was done in reverse. The time study man (work standards) determined the job content. The foreman would say to a man, "You have to do the job because that is what somebody tells me." So we had to get the foreman, with agreement of the general foreman or superintendent, to assume the responsibility. The foreman had to be sold on it himself or he would never get it accepted by others. We stayed with it. The time study man was there to measure results and to advise and counsel the foreman.

A change in the union's policy also appears to have taken place with respect to disputes on work standards. As one of the principal union officers said:

> It used to be that when a complaint came up, the union would ask for a detailed breakdown of the elements and time for the standards department. Then the union would check these against their own observations. Sometimes it took more than three months to settle it. We often said that we would have to strike the plant to get agreement. Now what we do when we hear a complaint is to take a quick look at it. If a man doesn't have a gripe, we tell him. If he does, we talk to the foreman and get it settled. So, management doesn't send the time standards men out all the time.

The Change Process in Retrospect—and the Results   **135**

This increase in interaction between members of organizational subsystems (production with maintenance, inspection, work standards, material control, and so on) is especially important in a complex production organization in which the technology itself demands a high degree of integration as well as differentiation (Lawrence and Lorsch[37]). Plant Y is a very large mass production facility characterized by continuous flow operations. As Guest[38] points out, a breakdown in any part along the flow could have, as it did in the early period of "disintegration," serious consequences. This kind of integrated technology places a high premium not only on speed and reliability of information exchanged between members of the different subsystems, but also requires exchange of information in anticipation of possible future technical problems. The social system of Plant Y and its functional parts are now behaving congruently with the demands of its technology.

Selznick[39] talks about certain "derived imperatives" or needs that are required to maintain a healthy organizational system. He describes

---

[37]Paul Lawrence and Jay Lorsch, *Organization and Environment: Managing Differentiation and Integration* (Boston: Harvard University Graduate School of Business Administration, Division of Research, 1961).

[38]Guest, *Organizational Change*, Chapter 9.

[39]Philip Selznick, "Foundations of the Theory of Organization," *American Sociological Review*, 13 (February 1948), 25–35.

The relationship of the work standards department and production foremen had become one of collaborative effort. The work standards department was regarded by foremen as a service, rather than as a control group. Foremen communicated frequently with their counterparts in work standards, and the advice of the latter was often accepted.

Maintenance

These activities were integrated with those of other departments so that the head of plant maintenance was no longer forced to view his services as a distinct and separate function. His primary concern became the solution of technical problems in cooperation with the other people involved. Information on which final decisions were based was exchanged at levels closest to the particular technical problem, then submitted to higher authorities as joint recommendations. The actions that followed utilized the specialized craft skills of the maintenance group, but the exercise of such skills was meshed with the needs of the total organization. Doing the "right thing for the plant" replaced what was formerly "doing the right thing for the department—the maintenance department." "Preventive maintenance" replaced "sending mechanics and electricians out on the floor to put out fires."

as "*homogeneity of outlook*"—*meaning that the members of the organization, regardless of their functional specialty, must have a common understanding with others as to what the fundamental purpose of the organization is or should be.*

These remarks by the comptroller illustrate that now Plant Y is operating as an integrated social system, that is, each of the parts— administrative/structural, decision making/information, economic/technical, and human/social (Hersey and Scott[40])—of the total system seem to be well managed as subsystems, at the same time effectively interacting with one another.

---

[40]Hersey and Scott, "A Systems Approach to Educational Organizations: Do We Manage or Administer?", *OCLEA*, pp. 3–5.

Comptroller

The comptroller's detailed comments describe not only what was happening in his department, but they illustrate the general pattern of change that took place throughout the organization:

> You know, most people in the shop always think of the comptroller as someone up in some corner office dealing with a lot of mysterious figures, and getting out financial statements, and making payrolls, and that's about all. This is perhaps common to the operation of any comptroller, but I recognized soon after I got to Plant Y that I would have a chance to do some of the things I long wanted to do. Matt Cooley told me right off that he felt that our department could be a lot more helpful to the operating people and the service departments. In fact, the way it worked out, Matt would frequently come up and grab me and tell me that we were going to take a walk through the plant. There were several weeks in which we went through the plant together two and three times a week, sometimes twice a day.
>
> I spent a lot of time talking not only to the department heads and the superintendents, but with the general foremen and all other foremen as well. I spent a lot of my time trying to find out what the figures that came out of my department meant to the operating and service departments, and then discussing ways in which those figures could be more meaningful. I tried to demonstrate what was behind the figures and how we calculated them, but it became apparent that, although they got to understand how the information on efficiency and costs and other things was constructed, they were not necessarily the type of information which would be useful to them in their day-to-day work. We found so often, when you really got the foremen to open up, they thought that some of our figures were lying. The figures in themselves were not wrong, but they certainly weren't useful to them, which amounts to

about the same thing. For example, if you simply come out with a figure and tell a foreman that he is 10 percent over standard costs, that doesn't mean too much to him unless he understands why. As we found out in our talks with the foremen, there could be six or seven different factors which would account for a foreman's being over standard, and some of these factors could be beyond his control. Yet he was being punished for them when they were beyond his control.

We worked for a long time figuring up a formula which the foremen and general foremen and superintendents could use to analyze efficiency figures quickly. Also, we broke down the efficiencies, after we got the overall figures, into individual elements and laid a program out on that basis. Next, we got all of supervision in and presented the idea to them, showing that the idea had basically come from our talks with them.

Our experience proved to me that a carefully devised system of financial control is not necessarily a real system of cost control. Real cost control operates on the philosophy that we adopted for the supervisors responsible for the different areas. In other words, the first thing to do is to get to know their needs as they see them.

A bureaucracy as described by Weber is designed to achieve predictability and "the highest degree of efficiency."[41] And yet, as Argyris[42] and Merton[43] and many others have suggested, the logical application of concepts of Weber's bureaucracy can create tension and stress leading to inefficiency, disintegration, and "dysfunction." Under Stewart, that is exactly what had happened in Plant Y. Now under Cooley, the organization was operating not only as a predictable bureaucracy but also as an effective human organization. In Barnard's terms,[44] Plant Y had become both an efficient and an effective organization.

With more information from the lower levels, those at top plant levels increased their position power at central headquarters. They were able to "sell upward," a condition not possible earlier. As the upward selling brought results from headquarters, those at lower levels became even more committed to providing reliable information.

Participation in decision making occurred at every level. No longer "selling" but "participating" predominated in Plant Y (Hersey and Blanchard[45]). The information generated was important data for the top managers who had to "link" with the division headquarters.

---

[41]Max Weber, *The Theory of Social and Economic Organization,* trans., A. H. Henderson and ed. Talcott Parsons (New York: Oxford University Press, 1946), p. 337.

[42]Chris Argyris, *Personality and Organization* (New York: Harper and Brothers, 1957), p. 13.

[43]Robert K. Merton, *Social Theory and Social Structure,* rev. ed. (Glencoe, Ill.: The Free Press, 1957), p. 123.

[44]Chester I. Barnard, *The Functions of the Executive* (Cambridge, Mass.: Harvard University Press, 1938).

[45]Hersey and Blanchard, *Management of Organizational Behavior,* 4th ed., Chapter 7.

Members of supervision reported that the new system introduced a degree of predictability that had not been possible before. As in the case of other changes that took place at Plant Y, the increase in the time perspective made it possible to plan, and such planning reduced the number of daily crises.

The increased coordination between the comptroller's group and other members of the organization had an important effect on Plant Y's relationship to the division. All of the major physical changes that improved Plant Y's performance involved substantial dollar appropriations and required approval of the division. The comptroller's department was ultimately responsible for "presenting the case" for division approval. The comptroller described how increased involvement in technical decisions helped him in requesting appropriations for capital outlays. As he described it:

I got into another kind of activity which is different from the kind usually thought of for a comptroller. Cooley would often bring me in when they were going to make some kind of rearrangement in the shop. Take like in the trim department when we made those big changes. I and my people would often go down as a group with Cooley and the heads of other operating and service departments. We would observe the operations themselves to see why the changes needed to be made. Even though I didn't know much about the operations themselves, I was always asked to express my opinion. My job, of course, was to work up the information to be submitted to the division for money outlays. It meant a lot more to us in writing up the request for appropriations, when we had the actual experience of seeing the problem itself and in having a part in making suggestions. In other words, we again got away from the business of sitting in an office by ourselves. We were cut in on the deal.

*Although substantial changes had taken place in the motivational "climate" of supervision, we find very little **expressed** change among workers. Unlike supervision there was little change in the intrinsic nature of assembly line jobs. The jobs continued to be repetitive and paced by the inexorable movement of the conveyor. It is true that some "hygiene" had improved. Some peripheral dissatisfactions had been reduced (tools, working conditions, and supervisory behavior). And yet, as Herzberg[46] would argue, the basic motivators had not changed. The highly structured*

---

[46]Herzberg, *Work and the Nature of Man*.

The Plant Y Case

By being "cut in on the deal," members of the comptroller's department were in a position to present a more convincing case to the division, and, as it happened, almost no requests were denied.

VI. HOW WORKERS VIEWED THE CHANGE

The focus of the Plant Y study is on supervision and management, not on workers as such, except for observations by union committeemen. Nevertheless, we were curious to sample worker opinions after three years under the Cooley administration. Just prior to the present case study, more than two hundred hourly workers had been interviewed for two hours or more in their homes. Questions were asked about job attitudes, supervisors, compensation, benefits, working conditions, and such.

A small sample of eighteen men from the earlier study was again selected for lengthy in-depth interviews. What was their view of what happened at Plant Y? Did they reflect the same "euphoria" expressed almost without exception by the management team? Had their behavior changed?

Following is a composite quote, made up of actual statements, accurately reflecting what most production workers had to say:

> My job hasn't changed very much since we talked last time. We're still fighting that iron horse (the line conveyor). It's a constant push. Finish one job and have the next one staring you in the face. You never can beat the line. I get real good pay. The benefits have improved. I'd like to find another job, but with my seniority, I can't quit. Has anything else changed

job on the line left minimal room for workers to realize opportunities for achievement, increased responsibility, and challenging work. The basic job design precluded one's ability to feel growth and "job-relevant maturity." This condition stands in marked contrast to what happened to those in managerial positions.

Although the workers did not seem to share the same enthusiasm that the management team felt about what had happened in Plant Y, there is evidence that the elimination of some of the dissatisfactions in the work environment stimulated dramatic improvements in worker behavior over the three years; that is, absenteeism, turnover, grievances, and poor quality performance were significantly lower.

Herzberg would contend, however, that only through deliberate efforts to redesign jobs by providing workers with a sense of responsibility and challenge could management tap the motivational potential. Herzberg calls the process **job enrichment** *(a term first "coined" by Guest in* **The Man on the Assembly Line***).* [47]

Turner provides the most complete diagnosis available of the feelings and perceptions of Plant Y workers in the post-Cooley period pointing out how the line technology and seniority system continued to sustain the workers' deep frustrations about the work itself and their feelings of being "trapped" in a system over which they had little individual control. [48]

---

[47]Ibid. See also Herzberg, "One More Time: How Do You Motivate Employees?" *Harvard Business Review*, 46, 1 (January/February 1968), 53–62.

[48]Arthur N. Turner, *Impersonality and Group Membership: A Case Study of an Automobile Assembly Line*, a doctoral thesis (Ithaca, New York: Graduate School of Cornell University, 1958).

in the last three years, you ask? Well, sure. The tools are better. They changed the layout so we're not falling all over each other. They got new lights, fans, things like that. Food's better in the cafeteria. My foreman isn't breathing down my neck as much as he used to. He lets me do my job. He'll listen if I have some ideas.

The questions then turned to opinions about the plant manager during the last three years:

I just read in the union paper that the fellow we had was leaving. The editorial gave him a big send off. Thanked him and wished him well. Never heard the union paper say that before about the top brass. Yeah, we knew who he was. I never talked to him much, but the boys thought he was a good guy. Didn't act like a big shot.

I suppose he was the one who changed things around here, even though it didn't make my own job much better. As I see what's happened in the last couple of years is that they took care of a lot of things that any damn fool knew was wrong—the layout, tools, stock bins, the schedule, line balance, safety, the fans, relief. We could have told them before, but they didn't ask. Yeah, now that I think about it, things are better—a little bit, anyhow. But, like I said, you can't beat the line.

Under Cooley's leadership, Plant Y had changed from an organization with not only declining performance but also deteriorating human resources to an effective organization in almost every measurable way. The general efficiency (direct labor costs measured against standards), indirect labor costs, efficiency loss and recovery in periods of schedule change and annual model change, and quality performance are all indicators that the output variables, in Likert's terms, were high, and the overall efficiency and productivity of Plant Y were at the top of all the six plants. Safety record, labor grievances, absenteeism, and turnover are all indicators, according to Likert, that the intervening variables were also in excellent condition.[49]

---

[49]Likert, *The Human Organization*. Plant Y would also be considered in good "organizational health" in Bennis' terms, because through the process of change it had developed a high degree of *adaptability* or problem-solving ability, it had a clearly defined *identity* that people at all levels could understand and accept, and it had well-organized techniques for *reality testing* to help its management perceive its world correctly. See Warren G. Bennis, *Beyond Bureaucracy: Essays on the Development and Evolution of Human Organizations* (New York: McGraw-Hill Book Company, 1973), pp. 52–54.

THE PLANT Y CASE

VII. PLANT Y PERFORMANCE—PERIOD I

There can be no doubt that Plant Y had changed substantially with respect to attitudes and morale in the management organization, if not among the hourly workers. The hard question, rarely answered in studies of attitude change, is "How did all this measure up in the hard facts of performance results?"

The "bottom line" figures speak for themselves. Here one can see not only what happened at Plant Y over time, but how it compared with five other similar plants in the division.

Direct Labor Costs

Direct labor costs had gone down 15 percent. Plant Y's position went from the worst to being superior to that of any other plant in the division. Although no specific figures were available, a rough computation of average wages and total man hours indicates that a 14 percent improvement represented a savings of more than $2 million in one year.

Indirect Labor Costs

The average cost per unit for the material and production control department had been reduced to the point where it shared first position with one other plant.

Quality Performance

The plant consistently held either top or second position in the division.

Thus, considering the basic purpose of Plant Y as a production organization, the evidence is overwhelming that a sharp, dramatic change took place when one compares the performance of Plant Y at the end of Stewart's leadership with its performance after three years with Cooley at the helm. Not only was there a substantial improvement noticeable when Plant Y's performance was measured against itself, but its performance, when compared with five (later six) other similar assembly plants, went from bottom to top position in most indices of performance. These comparative data are important as proof that the improvement was something generated internally inasmuch as all plants were subject to the same external market conditions. All were similar in product, technology, and formal structure of organization. All managers reported to the same divisional manager. In short, the performance change that took place in Plant Y over the span of three years can hardly be explained on the basis of chance. This all demonstrates that the positive effect of two significant changes in causal variables (Likert[50])—the introduction of a new manager and a change in the leadership style plus the behavior of top management in division headquarters (Cooley was allowed to lead; Stewart was told how to lead)—cannot be denied.[51]

---

[50]Likert, *The Human Organization.*

[51]In a study remarkably similar in results to the Plant Y case, Michael Tushman observed in his glassware plant that successful change was a sequential process in which structural changes (changes in the distribution of power) were followed by behavioral changes as a result of a Blake-Mouton type of intervention. The methods for affecting change were different in both cases, but the sequence of structural to behavioral was congruent. Under other circumstances, depending upon the history and the task of an organization, Tushman argues that the reverse sequence (behavioral to structural change) could be appropriate. See Michael Tushman, *Organizational Change: An Exploratory Study and Case History,* ILR Paperback No. 15 (Ithaca, New York: New York State School of Industrial and Labor Relations, Cornell University, 1974).

Efficiency Loss and Recovery in Periods of Schedule Changes

During the last year there were at least two major schedule changes affecting all plants. Both changes involved drastic cutbacks in production due to market conditions. When conditions changed, not only did Plant Y's cost rise less than did those of the other plants, but production "recovered" more quickly than any of the others.

Efficiency Loss and Recovery in Periods of Model Change

After the fall introduction of new product models, Plant Y came up to line speed more quickly than did any of the other plants. Also, during the three months following the introduction of new models, total manufacturing costs were 15 percent less than those of the next best performer and 50 percent better than the poorest plant.

Safety Record

Plant Y, having been near to the bottom three years earlier, now stood fourth among more than 126 plants in the entire corporation, a remarkable feat considering the potential for accidents was clearly higher in final product assembly operations like Plant Y than it was for many other types of production operations.

Labor Grievances

After the change, Plant Y's record was the best among all plants in the division (three grievances per one hundred workers per month).

Absenteeism

Plant Y's absentee rate (short-term personal absenteeism measured as percentage of scheduled work) was half of what it had been three years earlier.

Turnover

The average monthly rate dropped from 6.1 percent to 4.9 percent.

(If you are reading the case for the first time, skip to Chapter 5 and continue reading the case.)

chapter
5
Epilogue

What had happened at Plant Y was that Cooley and his management team had turned around an organization that had drained its human resources by extreme autocratic management techniques motivated by pressure from the top to produce. In its place, they created an effective sociotechnical system that was characterized by rational problem solving, participation in decision making, and delegation at all levels of the management hierarchy. While the change was drastic, it proved not to be short-lived. Since the need levels of people were changed from survival and security to desires for recognition and self-actualization (Maslow[1]), many of the new mature, responsible behavior patterns became internalized (Kelman[2]) while being learned. This automatically facilitated **refreezing** (Lewin[3])—the continual reinforcement of the desired behavioral change—and resulted in an organization that no longer needed a top manager who had to direct, control, and supervise subordinates' behavior. When the new plant manager realized that, he was able to concentrate his efforts in other directions.

---

[1]Abraham H. Maslow, *Motivation and Personality* (New York: Harper and Row, Publishers, 1954).

[2]H. C. Kelman, "Compliance, Identification and Internalization: Three Processes of Attitude Change," *Conflict Resolution,* II (1958), 51–60.

[3]Kurt Lewin, *Field Theory in Social Science,* ed. Dorwin Cartwright (New York: Harper and Brothers, 1951).

I. WHAT HAPPENED TO PLANT Y AFTER COOLEY LEFT?

After three years as plant manager, Cooley was promoted to division headquarters. The record shows that Plant Y continued to improve and that, for several years right up to the present, its performance record generally maintained itself in the higher rankings among all the plants. Cooley's successor had a markedly different personality and managerial style. One of his key men, who had been raised "in the Cooley tradition," observed later:

> At first he wanted to change things around using different methods to accomplish his goals. But he soon realized that our entire management team had learned new ways of being creative, of communicating, and of managing effectively, and he had a good thing going. The record showed it. So we were able to preserve what we had in spite of some initial "assaults" by the new manager.

One concluding observation: throughout the years, Plant Y had the same director of personnel, whom many considered to be largely responsible for Plant Y's excellent labor relations (union officials agreed). Plant Y had never "codified" in a written document what came to be known popularly as "The Plant Y Way." Several years after Cooley had left, this director, with the support of his present manager and others, developed such a document and used it for a variety of orientation, development, and training purposes. A key sentence in this 26-page document, called "People Programs at Plant Y," states:

II. SUMMARY THEORETICAL ANALYSIS
OF THE CONDITIONS IN PLANT Y—PERIOD II

Its performance during this period indicates that Plant Y has become a very productive and effective organization and is operating as a fully functioning and healthy social system. Its interrelated parts seem to be well managed as subsystems and effectively interacting with one another. What follows is a summary theoretical analysis of the conditions in Plant Y at this time. In presenting this theoretical summary of the conditions in Plant Y after the period of change, the same three categories used earlier to examine the period of disintegration will be utilized: (1) motivation and behavior, (2) leadership, and (3) change. Because many of the concepts have already been discussed, only brief analytical remarks will be made here.

A. Motivation

Maslow[4]/Hierarchy of Needs

Early in the change process Cooley had taken care of the lower level physiological and safety/security needs, which those in the management hierarchy were concerned about under Stewart. Gradually the management team developed a sense of cohesiveness, thus satisfying the "social" needs of the group. At this moment in time, in the bloom of success, most of the management hierarchy appear to be satisfying their "esteem" and "self-actualization" needs. The same cannot be said about the hourly workers, **at least as they perceived the change.** *Yet objective measures of behavior (absenteeism, turnover, quality work) clearly reflected some change in need satisfactions.*

---

[4]Maslow, *Motivation and Personality.*

158

CASE

> *. . . the strength of our organization is based on the ability of all members of the organization, both salaried and hourly, to communicate and draw upon each other's resources through . . . openness and involvement.*

These are only words on paper. But they have the Plant Y story behind them.

(If you are reading the case for the first time, return to section II in Chapter 1 and begin to read the case again, but this time with the analysis.)

Herzberg[5]/Motivation-Hygiene Theory

The hygiene factors in Plant Y are in good condition now, with many of the earlier problems with lack of job security, poor working conditions, punitive supervision, and deteriorating interpersonal relations being taken care of by Cooley and his staff. As a result, early in the change process the amount of dissatisfaction was reduced and overall satisfaction was increased within the management hierarchy. Motivators such as opportunities for recognition, promotion, challenging work, growth, and development were present. Workers noticed some changes in the environment, but these were limited to the hygiene factors.

McClelland[6]/Achievement-Motivation

Plant Y was now an organizīon in which people could satisfy their **need for achievement.** *Managers at all levels were playing a significant role in goal setting and in giving and receiving feedback on goal accomplishment. The various regularly scheduled meetings that Cooley established, as well as those that emerged spontaneously throughout the plant, provided the mechanisms for the goal-setting feedback process. As people began to get results and positive feedback, "nothing short of being* **first** *among the six plants would satisfy them."*

---

[5]Frederick Herzberg, *Work and the Nature of Man* (New York: World Publishing Co., 1966).

[6]David C. McClelland, J. W. Atkinson, R. A. Clark, and E. L. Lowell, *The Achievement Motive* (New York: Appleton-Century-Crofts, 1953), and *The Achieving Society* (Princeton, N.J.: D. Van Nostrand Co., Inc., 1961).

SUMMARY ANALYSIS

Homans[7]/Activities-Interactions-Sentiments

Managers and staff personnel were now engaging in a wide variety of activities and interactions that were both "required" and "emergent." The system created widespread positive "sentiments" at all levels of the management hierarchy. A good example of this changing pattern was the "blossoming" of meetings between operating and service departments. Homans would describe this phenomenon as "emergent" behavior resulting in positive and supportive sentiments (". . . just getting together as a group was worth something in itself").

Guest's observations of the interaction patterns during the "period of change" indicated that under Stewart's leadership:

. . . a far greater proportion of interactions had been originated by superiors and directed to subordinates than was the case [under Cooley]. In the first period a superior's stimulus to act was more often based on **his** superior's action toward **him** and not on the advice or suggestions of his subordinate, as was more the case [under Cooley's leadership]. In events involving production supervisors and their peers in production and nonproduction departments, the origin of interactions took on a reciprocal pattern. [8]

As a result of these observations, Guest concluded that the "period of change" was "marked by a greater 'balance' in interactions between levels and functions resulting in favorable sentiments and superior performance."[9]

---

[7]George C. Homans, *The Human Group* (New York: Harcourt, Brace and Company, 1950).

[8]Robert H. Guest, *Organizational Change: The Effect of Successful Leadership* (Homewood, Ill.: The Dorsey Press, Inc. and Richard D. Irwin, 1962), pp. 110–11.

[9]Ibid., p. 104.

Epilogue
161

Argyris[10]/Immaturity-Maturity Concept

Reactions of Stewart's subordinates tended to be passive, dependent, and subordinate. Cooley assumed these same people capable of being responsible and self-motivated. When they started to get positive feedback, managers at every level of the organization behaved, as Argyris would put it, at the mature end of the continuum, that is, being active, independent, having deep interests, strong commitment, and a long time perspective.

Berne[11] and Harris[12]/Transactional Analysis

*Behavior can now be characterized in terms of **adult** ego states (problem solving and rational decision making). Managers at all levels are seeking, giving, and evaluating information and looking for alternative solutions to problems. Life positions had moved from "not OK" positions to "OK" positions as the environment came to reflect open, trusting, and supportive behavior. From the very beginning, Cooley's behavior seemed to model "I'm OK, You're OK" feelings. For example, when he first met with all the supervision he told them candidly that he had heard that many of them were not capable of doing their jobs, but quickly added, "I am willing to prove that this is not so, and until shown otherwise I personally have full confidence in the group."*

---

[10]Chris Argyris, *Integrating the Individual and the Organization* (New York: John Wiley and Sons, Inc., 1964).

[11]Eric Berne, *Games People Play* (New York: Grove Press, Inc., 1964).

[12]Thomas Harris, *I'm OK—You're OK: A Practical Guide to Transactional Analysis* (New York: Harper and Row, Publishers, 1969). See also Dorothy Jongewood, *Everybody Wins: Transactional Analysis Applied to Organizations* (Reading, Mass.: Addison-Wesley, 1974).

THE PLANT Y CASE

B. Leadership (Attitudinal and Behavioral)

Blake/Shepard and Mouton[13]/Model for Managing Intergroup Conflict

At every level of the management hierarchy, the predominant attitudinal set about conflict seemed to be "although there may be conflict/agreement is possible." Conflict was no longer resolved through win-lose confrontation or through the "kick-it-upstairs" mechanism. Rather, conflict was handled by active problem-solving sessions involving all who would be affected.

McGregor[14]/Theory X-Theory Y

As suggested by the analysis of Plant Y using Argyris's Immaturity-Maturity Theory, the basic assumptions about human nature that emerged under Cooley were Theory Y. Although a few of the lower level managers suggested that their immediate boss had negative assumptions (Theory X) about people, everyone seemed to be identifying with Cooley and treating his/her subordinates as if they were self-motivated and responsible.

Argyris[15]/XA-YB

The prevailing behavior pattern among managers now seems to be B—supportive, "participative," general supervision. Cooley's comments and

---

[13]Robert R. Blake, Herbert Sheppard, and Jane Mouton, *Managing Intergroup Conflict in Industry* (Houston: Gulf Publishing Company, 1964).

[14]Douglas McGregor, *The Human Side of Enterprise* (New York: McGraw-Hill Book Company, 1960).

[15]Chris Argyris, *Management and Organizational Development: The Path from XA to YB* (New York: McGraw-Hill Book Company, 1971).

Epilogue

163

behavior suggest that he was a YB manager. Although he sometimes had to engage in A behavior—controlling, direct, close supervision—when there was a crisis or an emergency, no one seemed to question the underlying positive (Theory Y) assumptions he had about people. They assumed that he had a good reason for behaving that way. As suggested in the McGregor discussion, some of the lower level managers may have felt a pressure to use B behavior because of Cooley's modeling behavior, and thus were really XB managers. During this "period of change," there certainly did not appear to be any managers with predominantly A behavior patterns regardless of whether they had X or Y assumptions about people.

Tannenbaum-Schmidt[16]/Leadership Continuum

The leadership style throughout the managment hierarchy of Plant Y was predominantly democratic with extensive freedom for subordinates and little use of authority by managers.

Michigan Leadership Styles[17]

There was a high emphasis on both **production orientation** *and* **employee orientation** *in Plant Y.*

---

[16]Robert Tannenbaum and Warren H. Schmidt, "How to Choose a Leadership Pattern," *Harvard Business Review* (March–April 1957), pp. 95–101.

[17]D. Katz, N. Maccoby, and Nancy C. Morse, *Productivity, Supervision, and Morale in an Office Situation* (Ann Arbor, Mich.: Survey Research Center, 1950), and D. Katz, N. Maccoby, G. Gurin, and Lucretia G. Floor, *Productivity, Supervision and Morale Among Railroad Workers* (Ann Arbor, Mich.: Survey Research Center, 1951).

SUMMARY ANALYSIS

Cartwright and Zander[18]/Group Dynamics Studies

There was now concern for both **goal achievement** *and* **group maintenance** *in Plant Y.*

Ohio State Leadership Studies[19]

The predominant leadership style used in Plant Y was high structure/ high consideration and high consideration/low structure, with the exception of the production manager, who was high structure/low consideration.

Blake and Mouton[20]/The Managerial Grid

Plant Y management seemed to demonstrate both a high **concern for production** *and a high* **concern for people.**

Likert[21]/Patterns of Management

The pattern of management used throughout Plant Y tended to be **employee-centered,** *general supervision with little* **job-centered** *close supervision except when necessary.*

---

[18]Dorwin Cartwright and Alvin Zander, eds., *Group Dynamics: Research and Theory,* 2nd ed. (Evanston, Ill.: Row, Peterson and Company, 1960).

[19]Roger M. Stogdill and Alvin E. Coons, eds., *Leader Behavior: Its Description and Measurement,* Research Monograph No. 88 (Columbus: Bureau of Business Research, The Ohio State University, 1957).

[20]Robert R. Blake and Jane S. Mouton, *The Managerial Grid* (Houston: Gulf Publishing Company, 1964).

[21]Rensis Likert, *New Patterns of Management.*

In terms of Likert's continuum of management styles,[22] *Plant Y was now at the System 4 end of the continuum. This is particularly evident when one looks at events in Plant Y under Cooley in terms of the System 4 items on Likert's Profile of Organizational Characteristics instrument*[23] *(see Table 2).*

Fielder[24]/Leadership Contingency Model

The situation in Plant Y when Cooley first took over was **intermediate in favorableness.** *Although he had high position power (he was given a "blank check") and task structure, the leader-member relations between the plant manager and the management hierarchy had been poor under Stewart. Although Cooley started off with a "clean slate," he still had to prove himself to everybody. As his leader-member relations improved, the situation became very favorable for Cooley. He was even able to use a task-oriented style when necessary (often initiated by the production manager) without generating resentment from the subordinates. Generally, Cooley preferred not to use his position power and, instead, utilized a high relationship style.*

Lawrence-Lorsch[25]/Differentiation and Integration Model

Cooley, through the use of meetings and other means of opening up two-way and multiway channels of communication, was able to insure both the necessary high **differentiation** *between subunits and also* **integration** *among them. Now there was much more collaboration and sharing of*

---

[22]Likert, *The Human Organization.*

[23]Ibid., pp. 4–10.

[24]Fred E. Fiedler, *A Theory of Leadership Effectiveness* (New York: McGraw-Hill Book Company, 1967).

[25]Paul Lawrence and Jay Lorsch, *Organization and Environment: Managing Differentiation and Integration* (Boston: Harvard University Graduate School of Business Administration, Division of Research, 1961).

THE PLANT Y CASE

Table 2   A comparison between events occurring in Plant Y "after change" and System 4 items modified from Likert's Profile of Organizational Characteristics.

Likert's System 4	Plant Y After Change
Management has complete confidence and trust in subordinates.	Managers were actively involved in decision making through a variety of the committees.
Decision making widely dispersed throughout the organization and well integrated.	Management at all levels involved in long-range planning; foremen responsible for work assignments to hourly employees; all supervisory personnel concerned and involved in cost control.
Communication flows up and down the hierarchy and among peers.	Cooley present at initial planning meetings, and later, similar meetings are held without him; Cooley invites suggestions. Without direction from above, managers at lower levels start to "ape" plant manager's behavior.
People motivated by participation and involvement in: setting goals, improving methods, and appraising progress toward goals.	Subordinates feel top management wants them to get ahead; they participate actively in planning and goal setting; a free flow of suggestions.
Extensive, friendly superior-subordinate interaction with a high degree of confidence and trust.	Cooley visits plant to exchange ideas and socialize; well liked by all subordinates; no fear, high trust; positive superior-subordinate opinion; no scapegoating; promotion out of the plant not sought because of dissatisfaction but for growth and development.
Widespread responsibility for control process, with lower units fully involved.	Staff and line personnel at all levels take responsibility for quality control.

information than competition and "holding back." Mutual problem solving characterized the interaction between departments.

Hersey-Blanchard[26]/Situational Leadership Theory

Cooley started almost immediately using a high task/high relationship ("selling") leadership style, which was appropriate for the maturity potential of many in the management hierarchy. He provided direction through regularly scheduled meetings where he was also able to listen actively and hear about the concerns people were having. As managers began to respond to his expectations and performance started to improve, Cooley was able to change his style to high relationship/low task ("participating"); that is, meetings were being held where he could play a purely supportive role. The use of these new relationship styles was made easier for Cooley by having a high task/low relationship production manager on his team.

The high expectations that Cooley demonstrated began to lead to a self-fulfilling prophecy—that is, if you repeatedly treat people as if they are mature and responsible, they will tend to try to justify your high expectations; this will lead to higher performance, which in turn reinforces the high expectations and produces even higher productivity. Eventually, as time passed, the management of Plant Y was able to operate essentially on its own with little direction or socioemotional support from Cooley. He was able to delegate major responsibilities throughout the plant. As a result, even after Cooley finally was transferred (and for a long time afterward), the performance of Plant Y was able to sustain itself with little top-down pressure.

---

[26]Paul Hersey and Kenneth H. Blanchard, *Management of Organizational Behavior: Utilizing Human Resources,* 4th ed. (Englewood Cliffs, N.J.: Prentice-Hall, Inc., 1982), Chapter 6.

C. Change

Lewin[27]/Force Field Analysis

By getting managers at all levels involved in decision making and goal setting, Cooley was able to overpower or make driving forces out of almost all the restraining forces working against increased productivity. Cooley was able to get a "leeway to act" from headquarters, which reduced the top-down pressure and permitted him the time to turn around the resentment, fear, job insecurity, lack of coordination, and "buck passing"—all restraining forces under Stewart. At the same time, Cooley was also able to upgrade the quality of plant and equipment, and increase commitments to objectives and other driving forces.

Hersey-Blanchard[28]/Change Cycles

Cooley effectively used participatory change methods, which emphasize the use of personal power and general supervision, to improve the productivity at Plant Y. His strategy included: (1) buying time from top management, (2) promoting the identification[29] with a powerful and successful model, (3) restoring the hygiene factors,[30] (4) increasing his and his subordinates' "span of cognition," (5) restoring the use of personal power,[31] and (6) reinforcing successive approximations to the achievement of organizational goals.[32]

---

[27]Kurt Lewin, "Frontiers in Group Dynamics: Concept, Method, and Reality in Social Science; Social Equilibria and Social Change," *Human Relations*, I, No. 1 (June 1947), 5–41.

[28]Hersey and Blanchard, *Management of Organizational Behavior*, 4th ed., Chapter 9.

[29]Kelman, "Compliance, Identification."

[30]Herzberg, *Work and the Nature of Man.*

[31]Amitai Etzioni, *A Comparative Analysis of Complex Organizations* (New York: The Free Press, 1961).

[32]B. F. Skinner, *Science and Human Behavior* (New York: The Macmillan Company, 1953).

SUMMARY ANALYSIS

Lewin[33]/Unfreezing-Changing-Refreezing

Cooley demonstrated the ability to unfreeze, change, and refreeze the behavior of managers throughout the management hierarchy. This is evident by the way they continued to perform after he was transferred, without top-down pressure.

Kelman[34]/Mechanisms for Change

*Cooley did not use compliance as a mechanism for change, but he was effectively able to use both **identification** and **internalization** to engineer a signficant change in Plant Y.*

Guest[35]/Sociotechnical Cycle Theory

Measurable improvements in Plant Y's highly integrated production system were the results of mutually supporting changes in behavior (the social system) and technology (the technical system). As barriers to interpersonal and intergroup relations were removed, it became increasingly possible for its members to deal with technical problems in a rational manner. Sound technical decisions reduced mechanical breakdowns, equipment and maintenance difficulties, material flow problems, and so on. As the technical system worked more smoothly, it gave members of the organization still greater opportunities to plan and to interact under conflict-free circumstances. The change cycle continued with the positive cyclical interaction of social to technical to social.

---

[33]Lewin, "Frontiers in Group Dynamics."
[34]Kelman, "Compliance, Identification."
[35]Guest, *Organizational Change*, Chapter 9.

The Plant Y Case

part II
THE PLANT Z CASE

chapter
6

Introducing Quality
of Work Life
at Plant Z

Section One
Description of Events at Plant Z

I. INTRODUCTION

Although the evolution of successful change at Plant Z differs substantially from that of Plant Y, there are some remarkable parallels to be drawn. Plant Z is a unit of another giant American corporation. It machines and assembles a major component of a large consumer product. It is generally similar in age, size, and organizational structure to Plant Y. Also, it is one of several plants in a division of a corporation that operates many dozens of plants throughout the world.

Market conditions were rapidly deteriorating at the beginning of this four-year study, and a new plant manager had been appointed. Plant employment was down to 2,500 hourly and 435 salaried employees, almost half its full capacity of workers. Production costs and quality performance were the poorest in the division. Indeed, the new manager was told that Plant Z would probably be phased out within four years unless it could demonstrate a performance level high enough to merit a new product line. According to anecdotal information, the previous manager's leadership style was not unlike that of Plant Y's Stewart. He "went strictly by the book," using his position power to punish those who didn't "toe the mark and stay in line." He was said to have technical competence, but fear pervaded all levels of the organization.

The new plant manager, Tim Rafferty, had worked previously at Plant Z in a middle-management capacity, having worked his way up from fork-lift driver. He, too, according to a former foreman, "could ream you flat out." In his earlier positions at Plant Z he was respected for his operational knowledge. He admitted that he had been raised in an authoritarian mode which also characterized the life style of the entire plant and corporate hierarchy.

As he put it:

This corporation is a traditional organization and I've been a traditional manager. I like being the boss and I like giving orders and I like immediate response and no bull. That's been my style for twenty years.

Union–management relations were no better nor worse than in many other plants in the corporation. A brief wildcat strike had been called some years earlier. Many comments similar to a committeeman's "anyone with a tie, we didn't trust," were heard frequently. Whenever changes were made in a worker's job the automatic reaction was "to call a committeeman." At the time Rafferty became manager the workforce had been reduced to those with a minimum of fifteen years' seniority. "They knew how to hassle foremen and play the grievance game."

II. SUCCESSION OF THE NEW MANAGER

Just prior to Tim Rafferty's appointment as plant manager, the corporation and the international union signed an agreement that both would cooperate in a sustained effort to increase the involvement of employees in matters affecting their work—matters that were outside the collective bargaining process. This agreement reflected the concern felt by both parties and was needed to combat the threat of declining markets due to intense foreign competition. Foreign companies had found that improved quality performance and productivity resulted from involving workers in workplace decisions. The generic name for this employee involvement and participation movement became popularly known as Quality of Work Life or QWL, which is how the authors will describe the Plant Z effort.

Tough-minded Tim Rafferty was aware of these new developments. Frustrated by the company's traditional confrontational approach to worker relationships, he saw emerging in the agreement a new management philosophy. More important, he was personally frustrated with his own authoritarian style. Although successful in the past, it was not giving him personal satisfaction. He wondered whether this mode of managing was the way to operate in the future. He knew (and talked about it with his wife) that there existed a great potential for creativity among rank-and-file workers and his staff, if only they were given a chance. The company-union agreement triggered action on his part, and he announced to his staff and union representatives that the old ways of operating "are past and we have to take a new approach."

A month later he called a meeting of his top managers and the powerful and combative union chairman, together with two consultants who had long experience in helping organizations initiate QWL activities. Keeping to guidelines established in the national agreement, he urged that a joint union-management committee lay the groundwork for greater employee participation.

The union chairman, as he himself later admitted, was highly skeptical of the idea even though he was fully aware of the commitment made by his national union officials. Telling the manager and others in the group that he would "wait and see," he did agree to appoint some elected union committeemen to serve on a joint union-management committee. He acknowledged privately that he did not believe the company would change. And, knowing the plant manager from past experience, he was highly skeptical that Rafferty had had a real change of heart. What forced the chairman to go along was that something had to be done to save the plant. His constituents' jobs were foremost in his mind. He had seen plant employment reduced to half, and he knew that Plant Z was targeted for closure if performance did not improve.

In the weeks that followed, the newly created committee took shape; it was made up of six top managers (but not including the plant manager) and six elected shop floor committeemen (not the top bargaining committee). A line manager, who had some previous experience in QWL efforts in another plant, and the union chairman assumed responsibility for co-chairing the co-ordinating committee.

As the national guidelines had stipulated, the coordinating committee was not allowed to deal with formal contractual matters. They discussed plans for publicizing QWL, for communicating its purpose, and for implementing a structure for action. They asked for volunteers among the hourly ranks to form problem-solving groups. No limits were placed on the problems these groups would address, although the theme of *quality* (not productivity) was stressed. The groups were to choose their own leaders, were granted an hour per week "on company time," and were to be provided with a meeting room in the center of the plant. A letter went to all employees announcing the establishment of the joint committee and spelling out the philosophy of QWL. Top corporate, division, and national union representatives visited the plant to reinforce the importance of QWL and to show the managers and all union officials that QWL had full endorsement at the highest levels. Over a period of six weeks the plant manager held departmental meetings with all hourly employees to inform them of the economic status of the plant, to emphasize the urgent need for improved quality performance, and to express his personal commitment to QWL.

III. A CHANGE IN ORGANIZATIONAL STRUCTURE

Not unrelated to QWL was a decision by manager Rafferty to decentralize the organizational structure. He decided to divide the plant into two separate production areas. Each area manager would be responsible not only for the line supervision of superintendents, general foremen, and foremen but also for representatives from quality control and engineering. The latter two groups had previously reported to their separate staff function managers. The move was made, the plant manager said, because production managers had no direct control over decisions of quality controllers or engineering personnel, decisions that would directly affect the management of line operations. This structural change was to have a profound effect later in facilitating the QWL efforts of the hourly workers' problem-solving groups.

IV. SLOW START AND SKEPTICISM

Two months after the establishment of the joint committee, a survey was conducted to determine the impact of the many efforts to communicate the purposes of QWL at Plant Z. Most of the respondents, including supervisors and hourly workers, acknowledged that they had heard something about the program, but many were skeptical. This skepticism was expressed in different ways:

> *I don't believe management is going to let guys on the line have any say about plant operations. They have dictated things too long. You can't change a zebra's stripes overnight (a worker with 25 years seniority).*

> *We have had all kinds of human relations programs come down from the division and corporation. They made a big splash but then fizzled out. The top people didn't practice what they preached (member of the personnel department).*

> *This sounds like an attempt to do an end run around the union. I know the national agreement says that this QWL thing was approved by the union but we've been fighting with the company too long to believe they mean to cooperate (union district committeeman).*

Toward the end of three months the first two problem-solving groups were formed. They were chosen by the joint coordinating committee for several reasons: The hourly workers volunteered, and their foremen expressed interest; they were in two departments in separate areas of the plant; and the union district committeemen for these departments wanted to see QWL get off the ground successfully.

The group structure that emerged set the basic pattern for the more than sixty groups that followed during the next three years. There were seven hourly workers, their foreman, an inspector, and a process engineer. Union representatives sat in on the initial meetings as observers. The management co-chairman of the joint coordinating committee together with the consultants made a brief orientation about the purpose and process of QWL problem-solving. They were to choose their own group leader and select whatever problems they wished to work on as long as they did not concern issues covered in the labor–management contract.

In the first meeting and many that followed the temporary plant QWL coordinator (the management co-chairman of the joint committee) emphasized that the group was not simply to identify problems and then "dump" them on management for solution. Rather, they were granted both the authority and responsibility to come up with concrete solutions. If they needed assistance they could call upon those present who could provide further information—their foreman, the engineer, or the inspection representative. If necessary they could seek further information from anyone in the plant, including superintendents, managers, and the joint coordinating committee itself.

The reaction of the group members to the first few meetings ranged from expressed skepticism to enthusiastic support. Many could not believe that management would pay attention to their ideas. Others were concerned that the orientation had been done by the coordinator who was a member of management and they had yet to get firm endorsement from the union. Both groups "tested" the system by choosing one of their own hourly workers as group leader, not one of their foremen. Most of the problems they identified early were related to working conditions and environmental factors, but they turned soon to specific operating problems that concerned them directly. From their comments it was obvious that they were aware of the precarious condition of the plant, that unless quality performance improved the plant might even close down.

By the fourth month of the QWL "kick-off," other workers in other departments, hearing about the activities of the initial pilot groups, expressed interest in starting groups in their own departments. The joint committee agreed to allow five more groups to be established.

V. A CHALLENGE TO THE PARTICIPATION PRINCIPLE

It was at this time that another significant event occurred. A change in plant layout was being considered, involving the elimination of four assembly lines and building two longer lines in their place. The usual approach would have been for the engineers and management experts to develop the blueprints and then have the construction people make the change. Plant manager Rafferty, committed to the idea of worker involvement, told the assembly superintendent and his supervisors to meet with the hourly workers who were to run the new lines and ask for their ideas. The workers made many suggestions which were implemented. The operation started up with few hitches. As the manager of industrial relations put it, "In times past we have always been flooded with grievances and threats from the union when changes like this occurred. We learned a lesson this time which will set a pattern for the future."

VI. OFFICE WORKERS WANT PART
OF THE ACT

Another month passed. Word about QWL was spreading beyond the factory floor. Office workers made it known that they, too, wanted to be involved. Manager Rafferty and his staff recognized that the "total team approach" could exclude no one, not even those without union representation. On their own a group of clerical employees and a supervisor set up its own coordinating committee. They spoke with personnel in the staff and service functions and invited participation. One problem-solving group formed quickly and chose to develop a modernized word processing system for the office. They were self-directing; no supervisor was present. On learning that they were free to take whatever steps were necessary, they called in vendors from leading word processor companies, held hearings, developed cost estimates, and made a formal presentation to top management. The plan was adopted. As one member reflected,

> *We clericals were always neglected in this place. We didn't have a union to speak for us. And being women in a male-dominated plant we were taken for granted. Now we have a say. The real shot in the arm came when we heard that we were the first QWL salaried group to form in any plant in the entire corporation.*

Within a year several other white-collar groups were functioning; many addressed communication and information procedures linking staff operations with the plant production departments.

VII. A PERMANENT QWL COORDINATOR IS APPOINTED

As the number of problem-solving groups in the plant continued to expand during the next year, the joint coordinating committee, encouraged by the plant manager, saw the need to find a permanent coordinator to oversee the establishment of more groups and to provide orientation and training. The decision was made to select someone not from personnel or training as was usually the case in the other plants. An enthusiastic young man, well-respected in the comptroller's department, was chosen. He attended a division training program in group dynamics and was advised by the consultants on background issues and future perspectives. He conducted a two-day workshop on problem-solving techniques, attended by representatives of already established problem-solving groups, by staff support personnel, joint committee members, the plant manager, and supervisors in departments where the new groups were to be set up.

VIII. A MAJOR COMMUNICATION EFFORT IS LAUNCHED

In the weeks following the appointment of the full-time QWL coordinator a number of communication activities were generated and led by plant manager Rafferty. At every meeting of his staff and members of middle management, he voiced strong support for QWL. As he put it at one of these meetings:

> *We have to make sure that the guys out on the floor know that the top people here are supporting them and that we keep stressing the successes of the problem-solving groups we have going. We can put millions into systems and equipment, but only our people right out on the floor can save us.*

Rafferty mailed a letter to all employees outlining the general business conditions and plant performance and expressing his complete endorsement of the QWL efforts. The union and management co-chairmen of the joint coordinating committee sent a note to the six on-going problem-solving groups thanking them for their efforts. The letter was posted on all bulletin boards. One of the hourly groups also posted a note urging others to support QWL. The note included phrases such as, "We care, and we know you care. In the present crisis our personal and our company attitudes must change."

Word of Plant Z's progress in promoting QWL went beyond the plant itself. Members of the national joint committee, including a corporate vice-president and the union vice-president over all the company's plants, paid a one-day visit. Among the significant presentations was that of the powerful local union chairman, who had initially expressed skepticism about QWL. He openly admitted to the visitors that "attitudes on the shop floor had improved 90 percent." Two members from the shop floor problem-solving groups gave a straightforward, enthusiastic endorsement of their experience. The visit was covered by the local big city newspaper with large captions and pictures taken during a tour of the departments where the groups were active.

IX. A UNION COORDINATOR COMES ON BOARD

In spite of the surface enthusiasm by some during the first year, there were some problems. Less than 5 percent of the departmental units were directly involved in QWL. Few persons in middle management were participating in any direct way. Also, among the current problem-solving groups, there was some difficulty in stimulating staff support personnel from engineering, quality control and plant maintenance to assist in carrying through recommendations made by the problem-solving groups themselves. The most serious issue facing the QWL coordinator was "credibility." That is, he found in his orientation sessions with new groups a persistent, deep-seated skepticism as to his role. In spite of his statements that the effort was supported by the union, he was looked upon as a "management" man. Plant manager Rafferty, the joint committee and the consultants were fully aware of the problem but were stymied by corporate policy which held that although an hourly worker could be a "facilitator," in QWL he would have to report to the management coordinator. Rafferty, who had already ignored some other administrative directives, quietly passed the word to the joint committee to appoint a full-time union representative as the QWL co-coordinator with equal status. This appointment measurably helped to dissipate the suspicion of large numbers of hourly workers as new groups were formed.

I. NEW QWL STRUCTURE PUT IN PLACE

In the following months 20 new groups were formed. The two coordinators developed an elaborate manual dealing with every aspect of orientation, training, group leadership, guidance and project implementation. Initially the coordinators were critical of the consultants for not providing a complete training "package" and doing the training themselves, inasmuch as they were known to be experts in QWL. The coordinators in time came to realize that if they developed the training themselves they, and the personnel in the plant, would feel a greater sense of ownership.

The rapid growth in the number of problem-solving groups in the first year and a half (forty-three by this time) required an addition to the QWL organizational structure. The two coordinators simply could not handle all the training, guidance, and implementation follow-through.

One production zone had set the example by appointing a utility general foreman as a kind of minicoordinator for all six departments in the zone. This person, trained by the QWL coordinators, took on the responsibility for coordinating the six problem-solving groups in the zone.

II. ELIMINATING A LEVEL OF MANAGEMENT

Partly because of the success achieved in QWL in this zone and partly to streamline the organization, Tim Rafferty decided to eliminate the level of general foreman throughout the ten production zones of the plant. Each superintendent was assigned a staff person charged with a dual function: to act as a planner for the superintendent, and to serve as a QWL coordinator or "facilitator" for his zone. Not only did union and management plant coordinators conduct a two-day training session for these persons in their new roles, but a full day's session explaining the new arrangement was conducted for all superintendents, foremen, production engineers, quality control supervisors, and all union committeemen. Thus, at the end of two years almost everyone at Plant Z was made aware of the purpose and function of QWL.

III. PROBLEM-SOLVING GROUPS GET INTO ACTION

It was within the groups that substantial changes could be observed. No longer did one hear that management was dominating their efforts. They were "tasting" success and they sought more solutions. Whereas most groups in their early days tended to work on "creature comfort" problems (lighting, ventilation, etc.), the large majority came to deal directly with production problems. They were well-organized and set priorities. Minutes were taken at each meeting. Members were assigned to gather information and report back at the next meeting. Decisions were posted in the departments and copies sent to various persons including members of the joint committee.

As indicated earlier, each group had "support" representatives from staff functions such as quality control and engineering. The engineers were initially skeptical. They thought that hourly workers did not have enough technical background to solve complex problems of tooling, assembly, and the like. They thought they were being asked to "hold hands" with the workers when there were more important things to do. One incident was typical of their change in attitude. A young process engineer, who had openly expressed skepticism about the whole idea, said as he came out of a meeting with his group, "My God, those guys know a hell of a lot more technical stuff than I gave them credit for. They just solved a problem of machine coolants which the engineering department wasn't able to solve in three years."

The work groups increasingly found that they had the "right" to go to any source for information and action. In many instances they worked up a proposal with all the cost estimates for installations requiring substantial sums of money. They made formal presentations to high level managers, to the joint committee and to plant manager Rafferty, himself. Most of the proposals were accepted and implemented.

Two observations are in order. The first is that management refused, despite pressure from division executives, to impose progress measurements on the work groups. The groups were never told by higher authorities to work on a specific problem of concern to management. Neither management nor the joint committee kept records for the expressed purpose of holding the groups accountable for performance. The only discipline imposed by management was on managers and supervisors. The annual formal performance review was expanded to include the degree to which a member of management helped in enhancing the QWL process.

A second point is that in spite of the existence of a formal suggestion system, no group in four years filed a suggestion to receive a monetary reward for improvements made. Judging from comments by the workers and their union representatives, the most common expression was something such as, "Just being involved for the first time in improving operations in our own work areas is its own reward."

IV. PLANT Z FACES MAJOR CHALLENGES

Going into the third year Plant Z faced a number of challenges which would put strains on any organization. Based on a decision of the division and corporation, Plant Z was given the responsibility of making a product previously made in another plant many miles distant. This meant the transfer of more than 300 machines and the retooling of many more. Again, largely because of the QWL experience, the transfer and installation was not managed solely by the technical experts. Launch teams of engineers, supervisors, tooling experts, and hourly workers were set up in those areas where the incoming equipment was to be installed. If the set-up and layout was not correct, the hourly workers could refuse to sign the blueprints and process sheets. Rafferty acknowledged that the QWL experience made it possible to give shop floor workers both the authority and responsibility for final sign-off.

Also, during the third year, general business conditions picked up substantially. More than 1,100 hourly workers were recalled or newly hired. This required job posting. "Bumping" caused changes in the makeup of the problem-solving groups. An orientation program was set up for all the incoming workers. This included talks by Rafferty and the top union representatives. Many of these workers expressed interest in becoming part of a problem-solving process. It was discovered that the existing group members, according to one of the coordinators, "did a remarkable job absorbing the new members and getting them up to speed as problem-solvers."

V. FURTHER RESTRUCTURING OF QWL REQUIRED

The many changes that were taking place at this time, including the continued expansion in the number of problem-solving groups, put serious strains on the union and management coordinators and on the zone facilitators. There was no time for those responsible for QWL to service all the proposals for change being generated (more than 600 had been implemented or were in the process). Linked to this was another basic organizational problem which had disturbed Rafferty and the joint committee. Middle management and many district union committeemen were still not in the mainstream of the QWL process.

To address both concerns a mini-joint committee for each of the two major production areas was established. Each area subcommittee included the area manager, superintendents from the staff support functions, the QWL coordinators and some union district committeemen. They met bi-weekly and served in a coordinating capacity within their areas, linking themselves to the top plant joint committee. Thus a complete organization for carrying out QWL was put in place which was "parallel" to the formal organization structure. All parties were simultaneously involved in the dual function of performing their daily tasks and of facilitating the QWL process.

In another significant structural change in QWL, the union representation on the top level joint committee was strengthened. The plant bargaining committee itself took the place of the former group of lower level district committeemen. This move signified to the entire local membership that the union had made its strongest commitment to QWL.

VI. REORGANIZATION
OF THE MANAGEMENT STRUCTURE

Rafferty subsequently carried the team concept further at the highest management levels. He created what might be called the "office of plant manager," which included himself and his three top operating managers. He stated that henceforth all major decisions would be made by the team and not by him alone. (These men were also the management representatives of the joint union-management coordinating committee.) Each of the functional areas under the top management team was set up to manage itself as a team. Rafferty took the unprecedented step of eliminating the positions of plant controller and chief engineer. Thus, over time he had reduced the number of management levels from seven (when he took over) to four. The number of top managers was reduced from fourteen to six. In spite of the increase of more than one thousand hourly employees when business picked up, the number of salaried employees was halved from the year before Rafferty took over.

By the end of four years more than sixty-five shop floor problem-solving groups were functioning representing 90 percent of all production and service departments. In addition, a coordinator for the salaried and white-collar personnel had been selected during an earlier period. Almost a quarter of all such personnel were directly involved in QWL. Unlike the shop floor groups, which had remained essentially the same in structure and function, the white-collar groups included task force groups, participation teams, floor groups (supervisors and engineers) as well as various interdepartmental teams.

VII. PAYOFF IN PERFORMANCE RESULTS

What about Plant Z's overall performance in the four years following the succession of the new plant manager and the implementation of QWL?

In what is known as "labor and overhead performance," the plant improved on an average of 7.5 percent each year, the best performance of any of the seven plants in the division. The plant was operating at 80 percent of original design capacity, yet with only 54 percent of the original workforce. The most dramatic change came in quality performance, accurately measured by the number of rejects and repairs and customer complaints. Here Plant Z enjoyed a 60 percent improvement over the period of four years earlier. Not only was this the best performance among all plants in the division but, according to widely shared data, the best in any company in the world (more than 15 companies) making a similar product.

To all members of the Plant Z team the most rewarding fact was that the corporation, which had stated earlier that Plant Z was to be closed, now made it clear that its life was to be extended indefinitely.

Part of the improvement can be explained by the introduction of new technologies, new systems and improvements in design. But in the judgment of the plant manager, the principal cause was the implementation and diffusion of QWL. As he put it simply to a group of visiting executives, managers, and union representatives from other large American companies, "The QWL process is the primary reason for the success of this plant and my people." By this he did not mean the contributions of the hourly problem-solving groups alone, and these were substantial with more than 700 new changes generated by these groups. Rather he meant that the entire spirit of involvement and creativity permeated the organization so there could be dramatic structural changes in the management organization staff, changes that substantially reduced levels and personnel. As Rafferty explained:

> We simply learned how to use our resources better, and it was our own people from top to bottom who were involved in this change process. We still have a long way to go. There are still many dozens of people in here who are not on teams of some form or another. Our joint union–management committee is already at work on plans to radically alter the participation system so that every person in the plant, on a voluntary basis, can become involved.

chapter
8
The Process of Launching QWL

Section Two
Conceptual Analysis of Plant Z

I. PRIOR CONDITIONS

In many respects the conditions at Plant Z prior to Rafferty's arrival as plant manager were strikingly similar to those described in the Plant Y story. Thus, theoretical underpinnings lend themselves conveniently in making comparisons. For the conceptual references the reader is urged to review pages 12 through 22 in the section entitled FRAMEWORKS FOR ANALYSIS.

Plant Z was in deep trouble. In Likert's terms the critical indicators of performance were low.[1] The plant was in jeopardy of closing. The intervening variables, "that is, the condition of the plant's human resources," caused poor performance. Homans and others in the "Interactionist School" observed that human groups and organizations tend to develop negative sentiments about their condition when most of the interactions in a hierarchy are initiated from the top.[2] These were seen as punitive top-down pressures at Plant Z. The preceding manager was perceived by the subordinates as showing what Thompson would describe as "bureaupathic" behavior in which fear, mistrust and insecurity were pervasive.[3]

Although a full discussion of sources and uses of "power" are taken up later one can make the basic distinction here between what Etzioni describes as **personal power** versus **position power**.[4] Like Stewart in Plant Y, the previous manager at Plant Z, and, indeed, manager Rafferty in his prior behavior, relied almost exclusively on **position power**, the power based on position held in the organization and legitimized by higher authorities to induce others to act and to obey.

What McGregor would call **Theory X** was the prevailing set of assumptions held by the manager.[5] Because subordinates were assumed to be unreliable and motivated by Maslow's lower level **physiological**

---

[1]Likert, *The Human Organization.*
[2]Homans, *The Human Group.*
[3]Thompson, *Modern Organization*, Chapter 8.
[4]Etzioni, *A Comparative Analysis of Organizations.*
[5]McGregor, *The Human Side of Enterprise.*

and **safety needs**[6] *the appropriate behavior, so the manager believed, was to exercise direct and closely controlled supervision.*

As was seen in earlier chapters, the pattern of organizational behavior in situations such as that in Plant Z can be described as ranging along a continuum popularly described as **autocratic** to **democratic.** Vroom and Yetton developed a decision-making model calling one end of the spectrum **autocratic** and ranging through **consultative** and **group** to **delegation.**[7] *Tannenbaum and Schmidt applied the terms* **authoritarian** *and* **democratic** *to describe this range of managerial styles.*[8] *Likert found that supervisors with the best record of performance were those who tended to be* **employee-centered** *as compared with those who kept constant pressure on subordinates in a* **job-centered** *manner.*[9] *From this Likert developed his management style continuum ranging from a highly structured* **authoritarian** *style (System 1) to a* **relationship-oriented management** *style based on teamwork and mutual trust (System 4). Blake and Mouton's five leadership types included a* **task** *style (high concern for production/low concern for people) which aptly described the Plant Z manager as contrasted with a* **team** *style (high concern for both production and people).*[10] *In Plant Y's period of disintegration, the reader was made familiar with the Ohio State Leadership Studies which distinguished between* **initiating structure** *and* **consideration** *in describing alternative leader behaviors.*[11] *The Plant Z manager relied on his ability to insist on well-defined methods of procedure and communication channels. What Kelman called* **compliance** *best described the feelings of subordinates in Plant Z that one is forced to change by someone in a power position manipulating rewards and punishment.*[12]

[6]Maslow, *Motivation and Personality.*

[7]Vroom and Yetton, *Leadership and Decision Making.*

[8]Tannenbaum and Schmidt, "How to Choose a Leadership Pattern."

[9]Likert, *New Patterns of Management.*

[10]Blake and Mouton, *The Managerial Grid.*

[11]Stogdill and Coons, eds., *Leader Behavior: Its Description and Measurement.*

[12]Kelman, *Conflict Resolution.*

II. THE NEW MANAGER'S "CONVERSION"

New plant manager Rafferty openly admitted that he fitted the authoritarian mode when he took over. In his own words, "I like giving orders and I like immediate response and no bull. That's been my style for twenty years." It was the mode not only at Plant Z, but it characterized the entire corporate culture.

Why he changed his style and behavior, and did so in such a short time after taking over, is a matter of speculation. A behavioral concept developed by Argyris may at least provide an hypothesis.[13] Enlarging on McGregor's Theory X-Theory Y (which concerned assumptions managers make about subordinate motivation) Argyris linked these assumptions to a manager's or leader's actual behavior, calling this behavior A or B. An XA manager such as Stewart in the Plant Y case, not only made narrow assumptions *about his subordinate's motivations, but he be-*haved *in an authoritarian style. It is possible that new manager Rafferty was YA. That is, he basically held Theory Y assumptions but, responding to the prevailing corporate culture, acted in an autocratic manner, as he himself acknowledged. Only when he became frustrated enough, combined with the policy announcement of joint union-management cooperation through participation, did he "go public" about both his feelings and his behavioral intentions.*

Hersey and Blanchard's Situational Leadership theory may also help to explain Rafferty's "conversion" to a different leadership style.[14] The entire work force at Plant Z was made up of employees with long experience. They knew how to perform their jobs. To this extent they were at a high level of "maturity" in Hersey and Blanchard's terms. But they had not demonstrated the other element of maturity, namely a "willingness" to perform at optimum levels. Rafferty believed that they would respond, that they had the "potential" to respond, if he changed his own style from that of a "telling" style (high task/low relationship) to a more participative style. As we know from the case description there was an immediate and favorable response at least among those who dealt

---

[13]Argyris, *Management and Organizational Development.*
[14]Hersey and Blanchard, *Management of Organizational Behavior.*

with Rafferty on a day-to-day basis. It remained for the effects of this change in style to be diffused and institutionalized throughout the organization, a long process.

III. THE UNION REACTS

As the case demonstrates, the powerful union chairman reacted with skepticism to Rafferty's attempt to "sell" QWL. He could not believe after all these years of confrontation that management would change. He knew also that, as Maslow would describe it, his constituents were at the lower levels in the hierarchy of needs. They needed to feel more secure. The plant could shut down any day and all would lose their jobs. But it was this threat itself which caused him to "go along" at least tentatively with the idea of QWL. He was aware of the national agreement setting forth a policy of employee involvement and participation. So far, these were only words. Peterfreund points out that a written document put forward at high levels can be important as a first step, but the words become mere rhetoric "without consistent behavior and tangible commitment and support."[15] He also points out that a person such as the union chairman, in selecting representatives for the local joint committee, must consider that such persons may not be perceived as being "representative of all membership segments."[16] The need for building a sense of trust is essential. This is the heart of Ouchi's Theory Z: "The first lesson of Theory Z is trust."[17]

A key element in the willingness of both parties to launch a QWL effort was the agreement that contractual matters in union–management relations should be kept separate. Goodman's and Kurke's research in a variety of field experiences supports this. They point out that QWL is

---

[15]Stanley Peterfreund, "Managing Change: QWL/EI—From Launch to Orbit, Issues and Concerns," Occasional Paper, Stanley Peterfreund Associates (February 1983), p. 3.

[16]Ibid. p. 10.

[17]William G. Ouchi, Theory Z: How American Business Can Meet the Japanese Challenge (Reading, Mass.: Addison-Wesley Publishing Company, 1981), p. 5.

unsuccessful if union leaders are seen as "being coopted into performing roles [that are] indistinguishable from management."[18] The union chairman at Plant Z was concerned about this possibility when first approached. One factor shared by all was the threat to survival. As Pfeffer and Salancik found, "When environments change, organizations face the prospects either of not surviving or of changing their activities in response to these (external) factors."[19]

IV. ORGANIZING AND COMMUNICATING

There was no spontaneous and universal reaction to the pronouncements about QWL at Plant Z. The effort had to be organized. The joint union–management coordinating committee was formed to lay out guidelines and to communicate commitment. As Peterfreund points out, "Coordination of effort is vital: If a strategy rather than random activity is to be implemented, then the sponsoring parties must work through a coordinating committee."[20] The norms of behavior between two traditionally confrontational parties (union representatives and high level managers) began to change when they began meeting together on a regular basis. The increased interaction enhanced what Homans described as **positive sentiments**, even though tentative and exploratory at best.[21] Tuckman would say the parties were "testing" their opposites to "discover what interpersonal behaviors" were mutually acceptable.[22]

The manager and the co-chairmen of the joint committee led the way in communicating plans and commitment. For the first time in the plant's history the manager met with the entire personnel in small group meetings, using what Hersey and Blanchard would call a **selling**, not

[18]Paul S. Goodman and Lawrence B. Kurke, "Study of Change in Organizations." See Paul S. Goodman and Associates in *Change in Organizations* (San Francisco: Jossey-Bass Publishers, 1982), p. 16.

[19]Jeffrey Pfeffer and Gerald R. Salancik, *The External Control of Organizations* (New York: Harper and Row, 1978) p. 3.

[20]Peterfreund, "Managing Change," p. 5.

[21]Homans, *The Human Group*.

[22]B.W. Tuckman, "Developmental Sequence in Social Groups," *Psychological Bulletin*, 63 (1965), 384–99.

a **telling** *style.*[23] *His words stressed the new emphasis on mutual inter-dependence, "a collaborative process of goal attainment" in McGregor's terms.*[24] *At best he was trying to reinforce cognitively, through his presence and words, his belief in a more humanistic/democratic value system that had not existed before. In the face of an admittedly insecure work environment, he was trying to purvey what Argyris called a "psychologically safe" environment with emphasis on mutual trust, cooperation and especially the potential problem-solving capabilities of shop floor workers.*[25] *As Rafferty told plant personnel, "Only the people on the shop floor can save us."*

The same theme ran through all of the communication efforts— the letters to all employees, meetings with supervision, postings on bulletin boards signed by the co-chairmen of the joint committee, visits by top corporate and union representatives and notes from interested workers. "We care, and we know you care." As Schwartz and Davis found:

> Changing a culture is a complex long term undertaking that involves coordinated efforts by top leadership (note in this instance it included union leadership) to change their own behavior and the signals they send to subordinates. . . . Such changes must be reinforced by shifts in management processes, information systems, reporting relationships, and people's skills.[26]

Those attempting to get the message out were fully conscious of the resistance that could be expected. They knew what Lewin called the **restraining forces** *had to be neutralized and turned into* **driving forces** *for change. The change had to start with a process that* **unfroze** *the organization from its traditional rigid bureaucracy.*[27] *They emphasized*

---

[23]Hersey and Blanchard, *Management of Organizational Behavior*, 4th ed., Chapter 7.

[24]Douglas McGregor as cited in Warren G. Bennis, "Leadership Theory and Administrative Behavior," *Administrative Science Quarterly*, 4, No. 3 (December 1959), 259–301.

[25]Chris Argyris, *Interpersonal Competence and Organizational Effectiveness* (Homewood, Ill.: The Dorsey Press and Richard D. Irwin, 1962).

[26]Howard Schwartz and Stanley M. Davis, "Managing Corporate Culture and Business Strategy," *Organizational Dynamics* (Summer 1981), pp. 30–48.

[27]Lewin, "Frontiers in Group Dynamics."

The Process of Launching QWL **197**

that QWL was not to be just another "program" with a finite beginning and ending. It was to be a process of change *which would be diffused and institutionalized as a way of life for everyone in Plant Z. Or as Cole observed, ". . . Many 'programs' have beginnings and ends, but relatively few examples where participatory practices are highly institutionalized."*[28]

---

[28]Robert E. Cole, "Diffusion of Participative Work Structures," cited in Goodman, *Change in Organizations*, p. 173.

I. APPLYING THEORY TO GROUP STRUCTURE AND FUNCTION

Much of the success of Plant Z was due to the structure and function of the problem-solving groups. The assumptions behind their formation, how they were set up, what responsibilities they were to assume, all support much of the conceptual literature on group dynamics and effective group behavior.

When the first few groups were formed, and in spite of the initial skepticism of some, it was soon apparent that **groups** rather than individuals could be more effective in problem-solving. Maier's research many years ago substantiated this: "There is more information in a group than in any of its members. Thus, problems that require the utilization of knowledge—give groups an advantage over individuals."[1]

Theory supports the wisdom of allowing the groups at Plant Z to form voluntarily and to have control over the way they work. As others have pointed out, the level of commitment is highest when decision behavior is selected freely by a group and "not because it is an organizational requirement." This was the conclusion of Goodman and Dean after examining causes for success and failure in a wide variety of group participative efforts.[2] Successful groups, Tuckman held, "must decide upon the type of information they will need in dealing with the task, and how this information will be obtained."[3] Szilagyi and Wallace in their observations concluded that when higher authorities are willing to share power with problem-solving groups, "the group has wide latitude not only in choosing and diagnosing problems—but also in developing solutions to these problems."[4] The groups at Plant Z went even further. Not only did they develop solutions but in many instances they implemented the solutions on their own. Using a number of his own field

---

[1]Norman R. F. Maier, "Assets and Liabilities in Group Problem Solving: The Need for an Integrative Function," *Psychological Review*, 74 (1967), 239–49.

[2]Paul S. Goodman and James W. Dean, Jr., "Creating Long Term Organizational Change," cited in Goodman, *Change in Organizations*, p. 270.

[3]Tuckman, "Developmental Sequence in Small Groups," p. 386.

[4]Andrew D. Szilagyi, Jr. and Marc J. Wallace, Jr., *Organizational Behavior and Performance*, 3rd ed. (Glenview, Ill.: Scott, Foresman and Company, 1983), p. 523.

studies in QWL, Guest stressed the importance of this final closure, that is, of allowing groups to implement action:

> The essential function of the problem-solving group is not simply to come up with a set of recommendations for action by management. All members must be involved in working out solutions and taking action. What is not fully realized is how much a group is capable of doing without management intervention.[5]

This requires that management grant subordinates a broad **leeway to act**, as Guest pointed out elsewhere.[6]

The problem-solving groups at Plant Z initially lacked direction. Few members had experience in self-directed problem-solving. But once they had established their own priorities they demonstrated a high level of cohesiveness. Szilagyi reported on this phenomenon in the way groups functioned in the NASA space shuttle program: "If the group agrees on its purpose and direction of its activities, this binds the group together for better performance."[7] At Plant Z the group met for one hour every week and worked in the same departments, important points made by Szilagyi in discussing **frequency of interaction** as a crucial factor in maintaining group cohesiveness.[8]

II. SUPPORT PERSONNEL ENHANCE GROUP INTEGRATION

From the beginning of the QWL effort at Plant Z, problem-solving groups did not comprise only hourly production workers. They included representatives from the staff and support functions such as engineering,

---

[5]Robert H. Guest, *Innovative Work Practices* (New York, Pergamon Press, 1982), p. 16.

[6]Guest, *Organizational Change*, p. 128.

[7]Andrew D. Szilagyi, *Management and Performance* (Santa Monica, Calif.: Goodyear Publishing Company, 1981), p. 448.

[8]Ibid.

quality control, and others. *The rationale was that in bureaucratic organizations the separation of such support functions from the decision-making process can cause communication problems. Each works in a separate "box" on the organization chart, reporting up through separate channels in the hierarchy. This was dramatically illustrated in the Plant Y case during its period of disintegration and was also true at Plant Z.*

Lawrence and Lorsch saw the need to find mechanisms which would bring about greater **integration** *in complex organizations where* **differentiation** *of functions is created by size and complexity.*[9] *At the micro level, the Plant Z problem-solving groups served just such an integrative function. Peterfreund saw the importance of this kind of integration at the work team level: "It is not until representatives of these support services are integrated into the teams, that those involved in problem-solving begin to feel that the organization 'means it', and that their solution will have a chance for successful implementation."*[10] *Not only can the technical experts provide information to the groups, but, as Maier pointed out, "the ordinary worker can contribute to the engineer's knowledge."*[11] *Recall the engineer's comment at Plant Z, ". . . those guys know a helluva lot more technical stuff than I gave them credit for." As Guest has pointed out, the group sessions introduced a new form of interaction with engineers and others that carried over in day-to-day relations between staff persons and hourly workers.*[12]

An interesting fact about the composition of the Plant Z groups was that the foreman, although a member, was in almost no instance elected as group leader. This was wholly acceptable to the foremen. They came to accept the use of what Vroom and Yetton called the **consultative and group** *decision-making style for reaching consensus on solutions without dictating their own decisions.*[13]

---

[9]Lawrence and Lorsch, *Organization and Environment.*
[10]Peterfreund, "Managing Change," p. 7.
[11]Maier, "Assets and Liabilities in Group Problem Solving," p. 244.
[12]Guest, "Organizational Change," p. 110.
[13]Vroom and Yetton, *Leadership and Decision Making.*

III. EMERGING CHANGES IN GROUP ROLES

As the problem-solving groups matured in Plant Z they began to find solutions. A number of concepts can be used to explain this success. As Tuckman would recognize, "Their roles (became) flexible and functional. The group energy is channeled to the task."[14] *The tasks they chose to work on shifted from environmental concerns to more important issues affecting the production processes in which they were directly involved. Motivationally, Herzberg would see this as a shift from* **hygiene** *factors to* **motivators.**[15] *The groups moved from poorly defined and generalized objectives to concrete objectives, as Dalton put it.*[16] *As they saw concrete changes taking place as a result of their own efforts, they felt a direct positive reinforcement.*[17] *Lawler's research in participative problem-solving groups supports this. ". . . Change is meaningful only if . . . the change efforts result in actual changes important [to the group]."*[18]

As the technical problems were solved there were fewer breakdowns, hence fewer occasions for workers, their foremen, and others to confront one another in a conflict situation. Here is an example of Guest's sociotechnical cycle theory explaining the mutually reinforcing effects when **social** *actions (the group problem-solving) result in* **technical** *changes.*[19] *The solution of production problems reduced the number of emergencies and breakdowns, thus giving foremen an opportunity to plan for the future without having to constantly "put out fires."*[20]

Applying Hersey and Blanchard's Situational Leadership theory, it is obvious that these self-directing voluntary problem-solving groups at Plant Z had developed a high degree of **task relevant maturity.** *They*

---

[14]Tuckman, "Developmental Sequence in Small Groups," p. 390.
[15]Herzberg, *Work and the Nature of Man.*
[16]Dalton, "Influence and Organizational Change."
[17]Skinner, *Science and Human Behavior.*
[18]Edward E. Lawler, "Increasing Worker Involvement to Enhance Organizational Effectiveness," cited in Goodman, *Change in Organizations*, p. 306.
[19]Guest, *Organizational Change.*
[20]Ibid.

were on their own. No one in authority was telling them what they should work on and how they should carry out their tasks. For them, their superiors had appropriately adopted a **delegating** *style.* [21]

The same phenomena were occurring among Plant Z's office and salaried employees who had, with encouragement from manager Rafferty, formed their own coordinating committee to sponsor a variety of group problem-solving activities. As was pointed out in the case, the unusual fact is that these were the first plant level office worker groups to be formed in the entire corporation. From Peterfreund's studies of many American corporations, "with alarming frequency the salaried community is left out of the initial stages of the (QWL) process, with the result that their support and willingness to become involved later is tenuous." [22] *Again, according to Hersey and Blanchard, because of their high task maturity level the* **delegating** *style by management was appropriate.* [23]

[21]Hersey and Blanchard, *Management of Organizational Behavior.*
[22]Peterfreund, "Managing Change," p. 10.
[23]Hersey and Blanchard, *Management of Organizational Behavior.*

I. CHANGES IN THE FORMAL ORGANIZATION

Classical theorists in organization set forward some administrative principles generally considered to be universal.[1] *The Plant Z administrative structure contained many of the elements of these principles but modified them substantially. The* **Unity of Command** *principle, one boss for each subordinate, did not always apply as Plant Z changed over time. A QWL facilitator, for example, reported to his superintendent for his regular planning job but, when working with problem-solving groups, he also reported to the full-time coordinators. The* **Scalar Chain of Command** *principle calls for each link in the command structure to be headed by a single manager with clearly defined lines of authority from top to bottom. At Plant Z we saw that engineers held different lines of authority, depending on whether they were servicing agents to the problem-solving groups or acting under orders from other authorities. Indeed, production engineers "reported" to both the area production manager and, initially, to the chief engineer, depending on the task being performed. The management QWL coordinator reported to a committee (the joint union-management committee) and to the personnel manager. The union coordinator was an official in the union hierarchy and he simultaneously reported to the joint committee. There did exist the* **Span of Control** *principle, but it, too, was substantially changed. The number of workers reporting to a foreman doubled. Half the original top level management positions were eliminated. The number of management levels from plant manager to foreman was reduced from seven to four. The functions of accounting and engineering continued but with no controller or chief engineer—their jobs were eliminated. The office of plant manager became in effect a four-man team.*

Pfeffer and Salancik recognized the advantage of this kind of arrangement. "One way of achieving both accountability and adaptability may be to have . . . the actual organizational control lodged in a multiparty executive position."[2] *They also pointed out that the issue of*

---

[1]See Henri Fayol, *Industrial and General Administration*; Mooney and Reilly, *Onward Industry*; Gulick and Urwick, eds., *Papers in the Science of Administration*; Urwick, *The Theory of Organization*.

[2]Pfeffer and Salancik, *The External Control of Organization*, p. 276.

effective management is not "in assuring a concentration of control but, rather, whose interests are being served by organized coordinated activities."[3]

Burns and Stalker would say that Plant Z had shifted from a **mechanistic** *to an* **organic** *system of management in which flexibility of form and structure was required to meet changing conditions.[4] Reference has already been made to the concepts of* **integration** *and* **differentiation** *developed by Lawrence and Lorsch.[5] In the analysis of the problem-solving groups it was noted that they were made up of line and staff representatives to enhance lateral and diagonal communication to achieve integrative decision making. The same purpose was served through the team approach at higher levels. As Kahn would put it, some individuals served as* **internal boundary spanners.**[6]

These and other structural arrangements at Plant Z resulted in a highly **decentralized** *mode of operating. Both in the formal organization and in the parallel organization of QWL, to be discussed later, the power to make decisions was dispersed to lower levels. Design features such as the flat organization structure supported by the many teams, as Lawler observed, "all contribute to a felt sense of responsibility for organizational performance. . . . Only if they feel this will they be motivated to increase organizational effectiveness."[7] The record of performance clearly shows this to be true.*

The decentralized structure and the integration of effort in adopting an organic or team approach measurably enhanced lateral and diagonal communication. Guest called this process **enlarging the span of cognition.**[8] *Selznick called it "homogeneity of outlook."[9] This was important*

---

[3]Ibid., p. 52.

[4]T. Burns and G.M. Stalker, *The Management of Innovation* (London: Tavistock, 1961).

[5]Lawrence and Lorsch, *Organization and Environment.*

[6]Kahn, *Organizational Stress,* p. 101.

[7]Lawler, "Increasing Worker Involvement to Enhance Organizational Effectiveness," cited in Goodman, *Change in Organizations,* p. 286.

[8]Guest, *Organizational Change.*

[9]Selznick, "Foundations of the Theory of Organization," p. 34.

in a highly integrated production operation. A smooth lateral flow from incoming materials to finished product required, as Strauss emphasized, a high degree of lateral interactions, a knowledge of what others were doing along the work flow.[10]

Changes in the formal organization are only part of the Plant Z story. Also important are the evolving changes in the QWL effort and the way it came to be structured. The section to follow puts these changes in a theoretical framework.

II. QWL AND THE PARALLEL ORGANIZATION

To organize, implement, diffuse, and institutionalize the QWL effort, an entirely new organization was created at Plant Z. Heading it was the joint union-management coordinating committee, two co-chairmen, two coordinators reporting to the committee, three production area coordinating sub-committees, ten facilitators in each of the production zones, and more than sixty problem-solving groups with an elected leader in each. The salaried and white collar personnel also had a coordinating committee, a full-time coordinator, and several team groups.

With the exception of the full-time coordinators all members of this **parallel** structure performed their regular jobs as part of the formal organization. As such they played two roles: operating the plant, and unlocking through the QWL process the creative potential of plant personnel. The two roles were not separate. Rather they were enmeshed with one supporting the other. One might say the two roles were analogous to but not the same as Likert's **linking pin**.[11]

With a QWL structure parallel to the management line structure, as Peterfreund points out, "matters can be handled at the lowest level possible through normal management (or union) channels. The problem-solving teams must be linked in a communication network."[12] On the

---

[10]Strauss, "Tactics of Lateral Relationships," p. 182.
[11]Likert, New Patterns of Management.
[12]Peterfreund, "Managing Change," p. 6.

surface it would appear that the parallel organization was adding to the cumbersome bureaucracy, but, as Copenhaver and Guest found in their studies, "the evidence clearly suggests that the parallel organization enhanced the communication process."[13] In a different context Hrebiniak and Joyce stress the importance of supplementing existing "hierarchical channels" using teams to create new channels of communication.[14]

III. DIFFUSION AND INSTITUTIONALIZATION

As in the case of Plant Y it took a long time—more than three years—for Plant Z to become an institutionalized participative system with changed attitudes and behavior. Schwartz and Davis made this a central point in arguing that changing management culture in our complex organizations is a "long term undertaking."[15] In comparative studies of American and Japanese managers Guest observed that American management tended to look for quick results in QWL programs without fully understanding that changing from a bureaucratic to a participative culture is a long complex process.[16]

We saw at Plant Z that even after many months only a small percentage of the workforce was directly involved in QWL. A few groups had been organized. In a sense they were experimental and their survival tenuous. Many of the Goodman and Dean studies showed that early experimental groups rarely survive when those in the surrounding environment either do not understand or are hostile to the participative idea.[17] At Plant Z it took a long time to build a support structure at

---

[13]Lisa Copenhaver and Robert Guest, "Quality of Work Life: The Anatomy of Two Successes," *National Productivity Review*, Winter 1982–83, p. 12.

[14]Lawrence G. Hrebiniak and William F. Joyce, *Implementing Strategy* (New York: Macmillan, 1984) p. 168.

[15]Schwartz and Davis, "Managing Corporate Culture and Business Strategy," p. 47.

[16]Robert H. Guest, "Quality of Work Life: Japan and America Contrasted," *The Wheel Extended*, No. 4 (February 1984), pp. 8–14.

[17]Lawler, "Creating Long Term Organizational Change, " cited in Goodman, *Change in Organizations*, p. 308.

middle and lower levels. Also, the unionized workers deeply mistrusted management. The voluntary acceptance by newly formed problem-solving groups came only when a full-time union coordinator was appointed.

In many QWL efforts in industrial organizations consultants are hired to conduct training programs and to accelerate the diffusion process. Peters and Waterman observed that such attempts by outsiders do not often accelerate the process. They point out that the members of the organization "have to get into the problem and understand it—and then own it for themselves."[18] Peterfreund emphasizes that those involved in QWL must develop for themselves a sense of **proprietorship**, which takes a long time.[19] Because QWL at Plant Z was voluntary on the part of the employees, the process could be encouraged, as it was by the plant manager and the union-management committee, but it could not be mandated. It spread by what Guest calls the **healthy infection** principle, that is by word passed along that the problem-solving groups were both enthusiastic and successful.[20] Others "wanted in."

Even as the number of groups expanded it took months for personnel in middle management positions to accept it. Peterfreund warned against the "rainbow effect" where only top management (and union) and those at the lowest levels are involved.[21] But the process "bends around" those in the middle. At Plant Z it took two years to fill this gap through the establishment of coordinating sub-committees with representatives from key middle managers and union committeemen.

Diffusing QWL is a fragile process which can be threatened by external events. At Plant Z two major challenges had to be faced: to start up operations for an entirely new product line and to hire or rehire more than a thousand workers because of expanding business conditions. Despite the fact that workers had to leave their problem-solving groups and be replaced by others (as well as additions and shifts in production and staff personnel) the process held together. QWL had become, in

[18]Thomas J. Peters and Robert H. Waterman, Jr., *In Search of Excellence* (New York: Harper & Row, 1982), p. 53.
[19]"Managing Change," p. 6.
[20]Guest, *Innovative Work Practices*, p. 4.
[21]Peterfreund, "Managing Change," p. 11.

Lawler's terms, **institutionalized**.[22] *It had survived the crises. The constant* **positive reinforcement** *by the joint-committee and especially by plant manager Rafferty was crucial. As many scholars have pointed out, the continual expression of support from the top is essential.*[23]

The complete diffusion and institutionalization of change came not only from the successes of the problem-solving groups which eventually represented over 90 percent of the production departments (and the salaried employee teams representing almost 100 percent of the staff departments). It came also when most managers and supervisors felt that they, too, were involved and saw the benefits of the process enhancing their own quality of work life.[24]

---

[22]For a full analysis of QWL survival under crisis see Lawler, "Increasing Worker Involvement," in Goodman, *Change in Organizations*, Chapter 7.

[23]Warren G. Bennis, *Organizational Development* (Reading, Mass.: Addison-Wesley, 1969) and Richard Beckhard, *Organizational Development: Strategies and Models* (Reading, Mass.: Addison-Wesley, 1969).

[24]For a more complete development of this theme, see Robert Guest, *Innovative Work Practices*.

The Diffusion and Institutionalization of Change **211**

chapter
11
The Leadership Role

I. CONTINGENCY APPROACH TO CHANGE

Much of the research on the nature of leadership is supported by the empirical evidence in the Plant Z case and especially as one looks at the role of plant manager Rafferty. Today's theories reject the notion that there is one best way for a leader to be effective or that effective leadership depends on some vague notions of charismatic traits.

Scholars generally agree that effective leadership behavior "depends upon the situation." Whether a person is successful in influencing others is contingent on a variety of factors. Fiedler defines the favorableness of a situation as "the degree to which the situation enables the leader to exert his influence over his group."[1]

In his Leadership Contingency Model, Fiedler assigns three major situational variables that determine whether a situation is favorable to leaders: personal relationships, the nature of tasks performed by followers, and the power and authority as legitimized by the position one occupies in the organization. Essentially this model runs along a single continuum suggesting two basic leadership styles, those that are **task** *oriented and those that are* **relationship** *oriented.*

As was noted in the analysis of the earlier Plant Y case, Hersey and Blanchard expanded the contingencies into four quadrants along the task and relationship continuum resulting in four basic styles: high task and low relationship (a "telling" style), high task and high relationship (a "selling" style), high relationship and low task (a "participating" style), and low relationship and low task (a "delegating" style).[2] *In both the Plant Y and Plant Z cases it was clear that plant managers, prior to the successful turnaround of their organizations, relied exclusively on a "telling" style.*

But Hersey and Blanchard made the point that the effectiveness of these four basic styles is contingent upon the characteristics of those

---

[1]Fiedler, *Theory of Leadership Effectiveness*, p. 13.
[2]Hersey and Blanchard, *Management of Organizational Behavior*.

THE PLANT Z CASE

being led, the followers. Those in the organization who either lack the ability or are unwilling to take responsibility in a given situation are said to have **low task relevant maturity.** *The most effective style for their leader is primarily through one-way communication using a "telling" style. The appropriate style then shifts as the followers increase their maturity to the point where they have complete ability and the willingness or confidence to take responsibility. The leader's style synchronically moves from a telling, to selling, to participating, then to a delegating style.*

What we saw at Plant Z was that the original management autocratic style (one-way communication in a "telling" mode) was out of joint. There was a mismatch between the manager's style and the maturity level of the overwhelming majority of the plant personnel. They were people of long experience in the organization who had the ability to perform their tasks.

The new plant manager Rafferty understood this. He also understood that because of the long-standing sense of fear and distrust his people acted as if they were also unwilling to take responsibility. In short, they met part of the criteria, in Hersey and Blanchard's terms, for moving to a higher maturity level. When the signals came down from corporate levels that a more "participating" style was appropriate for the entire corporate culture, Rafferty jumped at the opportunity. His diagnosis convinced him that on the surface his people were unwilling to take responsibility, but a vast reservoir of potential was waiting to be tapped. They were willing and anxious to take responsibility if only he gave the right signals. Through his early announcements and frequent meetings he adopted a "selling" style. The results were enthusiastically received, enough so that he soon adopted a "participating" style. He encouraged changes in the formal structures and lent full support to the QWL effort which almost by definition required two-way communication and participation. Granted, the response in behavioral terms (performance) was not immediate. Attitudinally, however, the people in the plant knew they had the ability and felt confident they would succeed. In time, the problem-solving groups both in the hourly and salaried ranks demonstrated their ability and willingness to make decisions on their own. The "delegating" style of Rafferty and his management team became appropriate.

II. MOTIVATIONAL CLIMATE—PATH-GOAL ANALYSIS

Vroom's Expectancy Theory[3] of motivation and its later development in Path-Goal Theory by House[4] to explain leadership effectiveness can be useful in understanding why Plant Z was successful. Vroom held that people choose a variety of behavior strategies that will lead to rewards which they value, rewards such as pay, promotion, or recognition. If **effort** combined with ability is high, the results lead to better **performance** in the work situation. If the strength or **valence** of the reward for performance is high, then people perceive that the strategy of effort-to-performance pays off. Individuals may have strong feelings about wanting intrinsic or extrinsic rewards, but if they do not see the outcome of their efforts leading to a high performance level they become frustrated. In other words, they are not motivated to perform. In many respects the theory explains in part, at least, the low morale and low performance of Plant Z employees at the time manager Rafferty took over.

Path–goal theory links Vroom's theory to leadership effectiveness. It holds that certain situational factors get in the way of the follower's ability to be rewarded for effort and performance. The "path" is blocked. The leader can help subordinates structure the tasks (**be instrumental**), can show concern for the needs of subordinates (**be supportive**), can share information and encourage ideas (**be participative**), or encourage subordinates to perform at the highest level of which they are capable (**be achievement-oriented**). Thus, the leader, by various forms of behavior appropriate to the situation, can help subordinates remove the roadblocks and clear the way for them to achieve more effective performance.

As the problem-solving groups developed at Plant Z, they learned that they were capable of achieving high performance levels on their own, both in the decision-making process and in solving operational problems.

---

[3]Victor H. Vroom, *Work and Motivation* (New York: Wiley, 1964).

[4]R. J. House, "A Path-Goal Theory of Leadership Effectiveness," *Administrative Science Quarterly*, 1971, pp. 321–32.

Their achievement needs were not only fulfilled but strengthened. They came to have high expectancies and knew that their performance (instrumentality) would lead to what they regarded as most important—recognition. Rafferty as well as the entire structure and system of QWL helped to clear the path for success.

*An interesting observation about Plant Z is that the employees showed little interest in extrinsic rewards (i.e. the "valence" was weak). Much of the research in both expectancy theory and path-goal theory emphasizes the **extrinsic** financial rewards for performance. At Plant Z the rewards were **intrinsic**. Just the opportunity to be involved in the decision-making process "was its own reward" despite the fact that the problems they solved were worth hundreds of thousands of dollars in improved quality and efficiency—and they knew it. Lawler's research supports the notion that workers are not necessarily motivated to work harder and to perform better because the rewards will be to their economic advantage.[5] He stresses the successful appeal to a higher level of values involving democracy, equity, and the recognition of individuals as human beings.*

Another striking fact noted in the Plant Z case is that the results of the groups' efforts were not measured according to any traditional management criteria for measuring performance. The groups were not told that they were expected to achieve any measurable efficiencies through their efforts or that results would be posted and compared with the performance of other groups. Appeals for greater productivity were never made. In short, the groups were not competing against one another according to any preset standards. They were not being evaluated. Cole's long experience in participative structures in America, Japan, and Sweden supports this. "Measurement," he said, "has a strong tendency to turn into a punitive control system that discourages risk and innovation."[6]

---

[5]Lawler, "Increasing Worker Involvement," in Goodman, *Change in Organizations*, p. 311.

[6]Robert E. Cole, "Diffusion of Participatory Work Structures in Japan, Sweden and the United States," in Goodman, *Change in Organizations* (San Francisco: Jossey-Bass, 1982), p. 199.

III. LEADERSHIP AND POWER

Plant Z's ultimate success rested not only on matching the appropriate leadership style with the personnel's ability and willingness to perform. They had to perceive that the manager had the **power** *base to influence events. His style and the maturity level of subordinates had to be congruent with this accepted power base.*

What are these bases of power? If power can be defined as **influence potential,** *what are its sources? Starting with Etzioni's original distinction between "personal power" (a leader's* **personal** *influence) and "position power" (a leader's* **formal** *position in the hierarchy),[7] researchers have broadened the typology and thus expanded the contingencies.*

French and Raven's classification system is widely accepted.[8] It includes **coercive** *power (forced compliance),* **expert** *power (based on expertise, skill, and knowledge),* **legitimate** *power (one's position),* **referent** *power (the leader's personal traits), and* **reward** *power (ability to provide incentives and rewards). Collaborating with Kruglanski, Raven identified another power base—***information** *power (a leader's access to information perceived by others as valuable).[9] Hersey and Goldsmith added* **connection** *power (based on the leader's connection with influential persons inside and outside the organization).[10]*

Hersey, Blanchard, Natemeyer saw that the situational use of power could be integrated with leadership style and follower maturity. The various uses of power should vary with the leadership style according to the maturity level of followers.[11] They found that expert information and referent power bases, when leaders make diagnostic judgments, are

---

[7]Etzioni, *A Comparative Analysis of Organizations.*

[8]J. R. P. French and B. H. Raven, "The Bases of Social Power," in D. Cartwright, *Studies in Social Power* (Ann Arbor: University of Michigan, Institute for Social Research, 1959).

[9]B. H. Raven and W. Kruglanski, "Conflict and Power," in P. G. Swinge, ed., *The Structure of Conflict* (New York: Academic Press, 1975), pp. 177–219.

[10]See Hersey and Blanchard, *Management of Organizational Behavior,* p. 178.

[11]Ibid., p. 181.

appropriate for followers who are above average in levels of maturity (thus calling for a "participating" or "delegating" style). For those at the moderate maturity level, it is appropriate to call upon the leader's referent, legitimate, and reward sources of power. Followers at the lower levels of maturity require the leader to be perceived as calling upon reward, connection, or even coercive power bases.

Tim Rafferty appeared to apply these combinations of power, style, and follower maturity appropriately and effectively. He was admired as a person (referent power base), fully shared a wealth of information about what was going on at corporate and division levels (information power), and with his thirty years' experience in the business was perceived as a real "pro" in the business (expert power). He used the appropriate participating style and often completely delegated decision-making authority to his management teams and even to the hourly and salaried white-collar groups. On occasions he used his reward and coercive sources of power. The major change in assembly operations, for example, was initially resisted so he stepped in and called the shots. He virtually demanded that the superintendents call in the hourly workers for advice, telling them that a participating style was appropriate for them, given the expertise (high maturity) of the workers. He was able to get away with it because, as with Cooley in the Plant Y case, he had accumulated "money in the bank." That is, he had built up enough goodwill as a person (referent power) and, because of his extensive knowledge (expert power), the subordinates knew that there must be good reasons for his demanding compliance.

*One concluding hypothetical suggestion might be drawn from the Plant Z experience. Is it not possible that another power base emerged over time? By delegating authority to his managers and to the problem-solving groups, he came to rely less and less on any of the power sources centered on himself as leader. The source of power shifted to them. He "let them run the show" to an increasing extent with minimum intervention on his part. The power, in effect, came to be **diffused** throughout the organization. Rafferty himself implied that this was true. Because the plant had become so successful he gained greater power and assured Plant Z of a long term future.*

The authors had two purposes for sharing the Plant Y and Plant Z stories with management practitioners, teachers, and students. First, we wanted to demonstrate that effective change does not happen by chance nor does it take place because some simple set of causes has obvious effects. Organizational change is an extremely complex phenomenon. One must take into account a variety of external forces at work, a complicated set of internal administrative-structural, decision-making, economic and technological subsystems linked together through the actions and interactions of human beings who in themselves constitute what has been called a human/social subsystem. If the reader, through an in-depth exposure to this real life experience "in motion," has become more sensitized to these systemic complexities, then the authors will have fulfilled at least one purpose of the book.

Second, by sharing the insights of those who have studied organizational change and linking their observations, however briefly, to an evolving situation we hoped that managers out on the firing line might come to realize that there are available, in the organizational behavior literature, concepts and frameworks that might help them to do a better job. We believe that these behavioral science contributions might assist managers, in a variety of institutional settings, to sharpen their diagnostic skills and to develop appropriate change strategies. They might, in short, go beyond the intuitive, beyond seat-of-the-pants experience, to sense better the probabilities that one course of action will work and another will not.

In presenting a short-hand description of concepts and frameworks no attempt was made to critique or evaluate these contributions to knowledge. Nor did we conclude by offering up a grand scheme to serve as the conceptual model for dealing with organizations and the process of change. Rather we wanted simply to describe two good examples of what is "out there," link the description with a few conceptual handles and put the burden of evaluation in the reader's "court." Only the reader, who is now or who is about to be initiating actions in dynamic changing organizations, can determine how useful these theories and conceptual frameworks are. The test will come when one tries to sort out the myriad of forces, behaviors, and contingencies as a skillful diagnostician, then follows through as an effective leader, inspiring others to want to change and want to face new challenges.

Bibliography

ARENSBERG, CONRAD M., "Behavior and Organization: Industrial Studies," in *Social Psychology at the Crossroads*, eds. John H. Rohrer and Muzafer Sherif, New York: Harper and Brothers, 1951.

ARGYRIS, CHRIS, *Integrating the Individual and the Organization.* New York: John Wiley and Sons, Inc., 1964.

————, "Interpersonal Barriers to Decision Making," *Harvard Business Review* (22), 2:84–97 (1966).

————, *Interpersonal Competence and Organizational Effectiveness.* Homewood, Ill.: The Dorsey Press, Inc. and Richard D. Irwin, Inc., 1962.

————, *Management and Organizational Development: The Path From XA to YB.* New York: McGraw-Hill Book Company, 1971.

————, *Personality and Organization.* New York: Harper and Row, Publishers, 1957.

BALES, R. F., "Task Roles and Social Roles in Problem-Solving Groups," in *Readings in Social Psychology* (3rd ed.), eds. Maccoby, et al. New York: Holt, Rinehart, & Winston, Inc., 1958.

BANDURA, A., *Principles of Behavior Modification.* New York: Holt, Rinehart, & Winston, Inc., 1969.

BARNARD, CHESTER I., *The Functions of the Executive.* Cambridge, Mass.: Harvard University Press, 1938.

BENNIS, WARREN G., *Beyond Bureaucracy: Essays on the Development and Evolution of Human Organizations.* New York: McGraw-Hill Book Company, 1973.

————, *Organization Development: Its Nature, Origins and Prospects.* Reading, Mass.: Addison-Wesley, 1969.

BERNE, ERIC, *Games People Play.* New York: Grove Press, Inc., 1964.

BLAKE, ROBERT R., and JANE S. MOUTON, *The Managerial Grid.* Houston: Gulf Publishing Company, 1964.

BLAKE, ROBERT, HERBERT SHEPARD, and JANE S. MOUTON, *Managing Intergroup Conflict In Industry*. Houston: Gulf Publishing Company, 1964.

BURNS, T., and G. M. STALKER, *The Management of Innovation*. London: Tavistock Publications, 1961.

CARTWRIGHT, DORWIN, and ALVIN ZANDER, eds., *Group Dynamics: Research and Theory* (2nd ed.). Evanston, Ill.: Row, Peterson and Co., 1960.

CHAPPLE, ELLIOTT D., and CARLETON COON *Principles of Anthropology*. New York: Henry Holt and Co., Inc., 1942.

COLE, ROBERT E., "Diffusion of Participatory Work Structures in Japan, Sweden and the United States," in Goodman, *Change in Organizations*. San Francisco: Jossey-Bass Publishers, 1982.

COPENHAVER, LISA, and ROBERT GUEST, "Quality of Work Life: The Anatomy of Two Successes," *National Productivity Review*, Winter 1982–83.

DALTON, GENE W., "Influence and Organizational Change," reprinted in Kolb, David A., Irwin M. Rubin, and James M. McIntyre, *Organizational Psychology: A Book of Readings*. Englewood Cliffs, N.J.: Prentice-Hall, Inc., 1970, pp. 401–25.

DRUCKER, PETER F., *The Practice of Management*. New York: Harper and Row, Publishers, 1954.

EMERY, F. E., "Some Characteristics of Socio-Technical Systems," Doc. No. 527. *The Tavistock Institute of Human Relations* (January 1959).

ETZIONI, AMITAI, *A Comparative Analysis of Complex Organizations*. New York: The Free Press, 1961.

FAYOL, HENRI, *Industrial and General Administration*. Paris: Dunod, 1925.

FIEDLER, FRED E., *A Theory of Leadership Effectiveness*. New York: McGraw-Hill Book Company, 1967.

FRANKS, C. M., *Behavior Therapy: Appraisal and Status*. New York: McGraw-Hill Book Company, 1969.

FRENCH, J. R. P., and B. H. RAVEN, "The Social Bases of Power," in D. Cartwright, *Studies in Social Power*. Ann Arbor, Mich.: Institute for Social Research, 1959.

FRENCH, WENDELL L., and Cecil H. Bell, Jr., *Organization Development: Behavioral Science Interventions for Organizational Improvement.* Englewood Cliffs, N. J.: Prentice-Hall, Inc., 1973.

GERTH, HANS H., and C. WRIGHT MILLS, eds., *From Max Weber.* Oxford: Oxford University Press, 1946.

GOODMAN, PAUL S., and JAMES W. DEAN, JR., "Creating Long Term Organizational Change," in Goodman, *Change in Organizations.* San Francisco: Jossey-Bass Publishers, 1982.

———, and Lawrence B. Kurke, "Study in Change in Organizations," in Paul S. Goodman and Associates, *Change in Organizations.* San Francisco: Jossey-Bass Publishers, 1982.

GREINER, LARRY E., "Evolution and Revolution as Organizations Grow," *Harvard Business Review* (July–August 1972), pp. 37–46.

GUEST, ROBERT H., *Innovative Work Practices.* New York: Pergamon Press, 1982.

———, "Quality of Work Life: Japan and America Contrasted," *The Wheel Extended*, No. 4 (February 1984).

———, "Of Time and the Foreman," *Personnel*, 32, No. 6 (May 1956), 478–96.

———, *Organizational Change: The Effect of Successful Leadership.* Homewood, Ill.: The Dorsey Press, Inc. and Richard D. Irwin, Inc., 1962.

GULICH, LUTHER, and LYNDALL F. URWICK, eds., *Papers on the Science of Administration.* New York: Columbia University Press, 1937.

HARRIS, THOMAS, *I'm OK—You're OK: A Practical Guide to Transactional Analysis.* New York: Harper and Row, Publishers, 1969.

HERSEY, PAUL, and KENNETH H. BLANCHARD, "Life Cycle Theory of Leadership," *Training and Development Journal* (May 1969).

———, *Management of Organizational Behavior: Utilizing Human Resources* (4th ed.). Englewood Cliffs, N.J.: Prentice-Hall, Inc., 1977.

———, "So You Want to Know Your Leadership Style?" *Training and Development Journal* (February 1974).

HERZBERG, FREDERICK, "One More Time: How Do You Motivate Employees?" *Harvard Business Review* (46), 1 (January–February 1968), 53–62.

————, *Work and the Nature of Man*. New York: World Publishing Co., 1966.

HERZBERG, FREDERICK, BERNARD MAUSNER, and BARBARA SYNDERMAN, *The Motivation to Work*. New York: John Wiley and Sons, Inc., 1959.

HOMANS, GEORGE C., *The Human Group*. New York: Harcourt, Brace & Co., 1950.

HOUSE, R. J., "A Path-Goal Theory of Leadership Effectiveness," *Administrative Science Quarterly* (1971), pp. 321–32.

HREBINIAK, LAWRENCE G., and WILLIAM F. JOYCE, *Implementing Strategy*. New York: Macmillan Publishing Company, 1984.

HUSE, E., and J. BOWDITCH, *Behavior in Organization: A Systems Approach to Managing*. Reading, Mass.: Addison-Wesley, 1973.

JASINSKI, F. J. and R. H. GUEST, "Redesigning the Supervisor's Job," *Factory Management and Maintenance*, 115, No. 12 (December 1957).

JONGEWOOD, DOROTHY, *Everybody Wins: Transactional Analysis Applied to Organizations*. Reading, Mass.: Addison-Wesley, 1974.

KAHN, ROBERT L., and others, *Organizational Stress: Studies in Role Conflict*. New York: John Wiley and Sons, Inc., 1964.

KATZ, D., N. MACCOBY, G. GURIN, and LUCRETIA G. FLOOR, *Productivity, Supervision, and Morale Among Railroad Workers*. Ann Arbor, Mich.: Survey Research Center, 1951.

KATZ, D., N. MACCOBY, and NANCY C. MORSE, *Productivity, Supervision, and Morale in an Office Situation*. Ann Arbor, Mich.: Survey Research Center, 1950.

KATZ, DANIEL, and ROBERT L. KAHN *The Social Psychology of Organization*. New York: John Wiley and Sons, Inc., 1966.

KATZ, ROBERT L., "Skills of an Effective Administrator," *Harvard Business Review* (January–February 1955), pp. 33–42.

KELMAN, H. C., "Compliance, Identification and Internalization: Three Processes of Attitude Change," *Conflict Resolution*, II (1958), 51–60.

KOONTZ, HAROLD, and CYRIL O'DONNELL, *Principles of Management*. (4th ed.). New York: McGraw-Hill Book Company, 1968.

KORMAN, A. K. " 'Consideration,' 'Initiating Structure,' and Organizational Criteria—A Review," *Personnel Psychology: A Journal of Applied Research*, XIX, No. 4 (Winter 1966), 349–61.

LAWLER, EDWARD E., "Increasing Worker Involvement to Enhance Organizational Effectiveness," cited in Goodman, *Change in Organizations*.

———, "Creating Long Term Organizational Change," cited in Goodman, *Change in Organizations*.

LAWRENCE, PAUL, and JAY LORSCH, *Organization and Environment: Managing Differentiation and Integration*. Boston: Harvard University, Graduate School of Business Administration, Division of Research, 1961.

LEAVITT, HAROLD J., "Applied Organizational Change in Industry: Structural, Technological and Humanistic Approaches," in *Handbook of Organizations*, ed. James G. March. New York: Rand McNally and Co., 1965.

LEWIN, KURT, "Frontiers in Group Dynamics: Concept, Method, and Reality in Social Science, Social Equilibria and Social Change." *Human Relations*, I, No. 1 (June 1947), 5–41.

———, "Psychology of Success and Failure," *Occupations*, 14 (June 1936), 926–30.

LIKERT, RENSIS, *The Human Organizations*. New York: McGraw-Hill Book Company, 1969.

———, *New Patterns of Management*. New York: McGraw-Hill Book Company, 1961.

LITTERER, JOSEPH A., *The Analysis of Organizations* (2nd ed.). New York: John Wiley and Sons, Inc., 1975.

LUFT, JOSEPH, *Group Process* (2nd ed.). Palo Alto, Calif.: National Press Book, 1970.

LUFT, JOSEPH, and HARRY INGHAM, "The Johari Window, a Graphic Model of Interpersonal Awareness," *Proceedings of the Western Training Laboratory in Group Development*. Los Angeles: University of California, Extension Office (August, 1955). See also, *Human Relations Training News*. Washington D.C.: National Education Association, 5, No. 1 (1961).

MAIER, NORMAN R. F., "Assets and Liabilities in Group Problem Solving: The Need for an Integrative Function," *Psychological Review*, 74, 1967.

McCLELLAND, DAVID, et al., *The Achievement Motive*. New York: Appleton-Century-Crofts, 1953.

————, *The Achieving Society*. Princeton, N. J.: D. Van Nostrand Co., Inc., 1961.

McGREGOR, DOUGLAS, *The Human Side of Enterprise*. New York: McGraw-Hill Book Company, 1960.

————, as cited in Warren G. Bennis, "Leadership Theory and Administrative Behavior," *Administrative Science Quarterly*, 4, No. 3 (December 1959), 259–301.

MACHIAVELLI, NICCOLÒ, *The Prince*. Northbrook, Ill.: AHM Publishing Corporation, 1947.

MASLOW, ABRAHAM H., *Motivation and Personality*. New York: Harper and Row, Publishers, 1954.

MERTON, ROBERT K., *Social Theory and Social Structure* (rev. ed.). Glencoe, Ill.: The Free Press, 1957.

MERTON, ROBERT K., et al., eds., *Reader in Bureaucracy*. Glencoe, Ill.: The Free Press, 1952.

MILES, RAYMOND E., "Human Relations or Human Resources," *Harvard Business Review* (July–August 1965).

MOONEY, J. D., and A. C. REILEY, *Onward Industry*. New York: Harper and Brothers, 1931.

————, *The Principles of Organization*. New York: Harper and Brothers, 1939.

OUCHI, WILLIAM G., *Theory Z: How American Business Can Meet the Japanese Challenge*. Reading, Mass.: Addison-Wesley, 1981.

ODIORNE, GEORGE S., *Management of Objectives*. New York: Pitman Publishing Corp., 1965.

PETERFREUND, STANLEY, "Managing Change: QWL/EI—From Launch to Orbit, Issues and Concerns," Occasional Paper, Stanley Peterfreund Associates, February 1983.

PETERS, THOMAS J., and ROBERT H. WATERMAN, JR., *In Search of Excellence*. New York: Harper & Row, 1982.

PFEFFER, JEFFREY, and GERALD R. SALANCIK, *The External Control of Organizations*. New York: Harper and Row, 1978.

RAVEN, B. H., and W. KRUGLANSKI, "Conflict and Power," in P. G. Swingle, ed., *The Structure of Conflict*. New York: Academic Press, 1975, 177–219.

RICHARDSON, FREDERICK L. W., and CHARLES R. WALKER, *Human Relations in an Expanding Company*. New Haven: Yale University, Labor and Management Center, 1948.

SCHEIN, EDGAR H., "Management Development as a Process of Influence," *Industrial Management Review*, II (May 1961).

———, *Organizational Psychology* (2nd ed.). Englewood Cliffs, N.J.: Prentice-Hall, Inc., 1970.

SCHWARTZ, HOWARD, and STANLEY M. DAVIS, "Managing Corporate Culture and Business Strategy," *Organizational Dynamics*. Summer 1981, pp. 30–48.

SEILER, JOHN A., *Systems Analysis in Organizational Behavior*. Homewood, Ill.: Richard D. Irwin, Inc., 1967.

SELZNICK, PHILIP, "Foundations of the Theory of Organization," *American Sociological Review*, 13 (February 1948), 25–35.

SKINNER, B. F., *Science and Human Behavior*. New York: The Macmillan Company, 1953.

STOGDILL, ROGER M., and ALVIN E. COONS, eds., *Leader Behavior: Its Description and Measurement*. Research Monograph No. 88. Columbus: The Ohio State University, Bureau of Business Research, 1957.

STRAUSS, GEORGE, "Tactics of Lateral Relationship: The Purchasing Agent," *Administrative Science Quarterly*, 7, No. 2 (September 1962), 161–86.

SZILAGYI, ANDREW D., JR., *Management and Performance*. Santa Monica, Calif: Goodyear Publishing Company, 1981.

SZILAGYI, ANDREW D., JR., and MARC J. WALLACE, JR., *Organizational Behavior and Performance* (3rd ed.). Glenview, Ill.: Scott, Foresman and Company, 1983.

TANNENBAUM, ROBERT, and WARREN H. SCHMIDT, "How to Choose a Leadership Pattern," *Harvard Business Review* (March–April 1957), pp. 95–101.

THOMPSON, VICTOR A., *Modern Organization*. New York: Alfred A. Knopf, Inc., 1961.

TRIST, E. L., and K. W. BANFORD, "Some Social and Psychological Consequences of the Long Wall Method of Coal Getting," *Human Relations*, 4, No. 1 (1951), 3–38.

TRIST, E. L., et al., *Organizational Choice*. London: Tavistock Publications, 1963.

TUCKMAN, B. W., "Developmental Sequence in Social Groups," *Psychological Bulletin*, 63 (1965), 384–99.

TURNER, ARTHUR N., *Impersonality and Group Membership: A Case Study of an Automobile Assembly Line*, a doctoral thesis (Ithaca, N.Y.: Graduate School of Cornell University, 1958).

————, "Management and the Assembly Line," *Harvard Business Review* (September-October 1955), pp. 40–48.

TUSHMAN, MICHAEL, *Organizational Change: An Exploratory Study and Case History*, ILR Paperback No. 15 (Ithaca, N.Y.: Cornell University, New York State School of Industrial and Labor Relations, 1974).

URWICK, LYNDALL F., *The Theory of Organization*. New York: American Management Association, 1952.

Vroom, Victor H., *Work and Motivation*. New York: John Wiley and Sons, Inc., 1964.

VROOM, VICTOR H., and PHILIP YETTON, *Leadership and Decision Making*. Pittsburgh: University of Pittsburgh Press, 1973.

WALKER, CHARLES R., and ROBERT H. GUEST, *The Man on the Assembly Line*. Cambridge: Harvard University Press, 1952.

WEBBER, ROSS A., *Management: Basic Elements of Managing Organizations*. Homewood, Ill.: Richard D. Irwin, Inc., 1975.

WEBER, MAX, *The Theory of Social and Economic Organization*, trans. A. H. Henderson and ed. Talcott Parsons. New York: Oxford University Press, 1946.

WHYTE, WILLIAM F., "Framework for the Analysis of Industrial Relations," *Industrial and Labor Relations Review*, Vol. 3, No. 3 (April 1950).

Author Index

Peters, T. J., 210
Pfeffer, J., 196, 206

R

Raven, B. H., 30, 218
Reiley, A. C., 38, 82
Richardson, F. L. W., 24

S

Salancik, G. R., 196, 206
Schein, E. H., 5, 104
Schmidt, W. H., 63, 164, 193
Schwartz, H., 197, 209
Scott, D., 13, 46, 138
Seiler, J. A., 13
Selznick, P., 136, 207
Shepard, H., 48, 62, 128, 163
Skinner, B. F., 96, 122, 169, 203
Stalker, G. M., 207
Stogdill, R. M., 64, 165, 193
Strauss, G., 126, 207
Szilagi, A. D., Jr., 200, 201

T

Tannenbaum, R., 63, 164, 193
Thompson, V. A., 28, 192
Thorsrud, E., 22
Trist, E. L., 21

Tuckman, B. W., 196, 200, 203
Turner, A. N., 22, 146
Tushman, M., 150

U

Urwick, L. F., 38

V

Vroom, V. H., 50, 80, 98, 130, 134, 193, 202, 216

W

Walker, C. R., 22, 24
Wallace, M. J., Jr., 200
Waterman, R. H., 210
Webber, R. A., 40
Weber, M., 14, 142
Whyte, W. F., 24

Y

Yavitz, B., 13
Yetton, P., 50, 80, 98, 130, 134, 193, 202

Z

Zander, A., 64, 165